LANCHESTER LIBRARY

D0271032

LANCHESTER LIBRARY

D0271032

Everyday Details

EVERYDAY DETAILS

Cecil C. Handisyde

ARIBA, AADip

Butterworth Architecture
London Boston Singapore Sydney Toronto Wellington

Coventry University Library

Butterworth Architecture
is an imprint of Butterworth Scientific

All rights reserved. No part of this publication may be reproduced or
transmitted in any form or by any means, including photocopying and
recording, without the written permission of the copyright holder,
application for which should be addressed to the Publishers, or in
accordance with the provisions of the Copyright Act 1956 (as
ammended), or under the terms of any licence permitting limited
copying issued by the Copyright Licensing Agency, 7 Ridgemount
Street, London WC1E 7AE, England. Such written permission must
also be obtained before any part of this publication is stored in a
retrieval system of any nature.

Any person who does any unauthorized act in relation to this
publication may be liable to criminal prosecution and civil claims for
damages.

This book is sold subject to the Standard Conditions of Sale of Net
Books and may not be re-sold in the UK below the net price given by
the Publishers in their current price list.

© **Butterworth & Co (Publishers) Ltd, 1976**
ISBN 0-85139-213-X

First published in book form in 1976 by
The Architectural Press Ltd, London
Reprinted 1977, 1978, 1980, 1981, 1984, 1988

Coventry University Library

Printed and bound in Great Britain by
Anchor Brendon Ltd, Tiptree, Essex

Contents

Foreword

In 1923 The Architectural Press published a delightful and useful little book, written by an architect named Edwin Gunn, called *Little Things That Matter For Those Who Build*.* It did not claim, in its 82 pages, to do more than give a practical man's view on the real problems of putting a simple, traditional building together. It was never intended to be—and this was its great strength—an exhaustive treatise on building construction. Its style was informal and chatty and the author was never one to shrink from giving a frank opinion—'that execrable material, black mortar . . .'—or from being whimsical, **1**. But his intentions were serious and his advice sound, **2**.

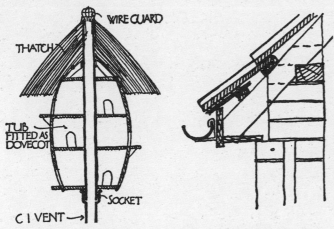

1 *Gunn's whimsical dovecote.* **2** *Gunn's recommended eaves.*

Fifty years later, in 1973, *The Architects' Journal* started a series of studies along similar lines, and it is from these studies and from the dialogue they provoked that this book is compiled. Some traditional building techniques have not changed radically since Gunn set down his experience for his colleagues to share. But, after half a century, there are many instances where changes and developments in basic materials and standards of design have progressed beyond the boundaries of his book. *Everyday Details* sets out to tackle problems in detailing, from foundations to roof, and gives information and advice on good, sound current practice applicable to small two- and three-storey structures: the sort of work which forms the bulk of many practices.

Good (and sometimes bad) ways of detailing each building element are described in brief explanatory notes, illustrated by sketches isolating particular trouble spots. The details are not intended as 'standard details', to be traced off and used directly on a set of working drawings. They are intended to pinpoint those parts of a building which, small in themselves, are nevertheless frequent sources of failure. The book should prove especially useful to young architects with limited site experience, and to students with little training in practical building.

In the introduction to the Everyday Details published in *The Architects' Journal*, the editor said: 'Many experienced architects will perhaps despair that the series is necessary at all. Others may disagree with particular details shown—we hope they will write and tell us so.'

The series did produce a considerable amount of comment and many constructive suggestions. These have been incorporated into this book, together with, in some cases, editorial replies to

*No longer in print

the comments. Despite extensive discussion of drafts by the original team, followed by submission of their work to at least two other experts for further checking and comment prior to publication, readers were able to point out a few errors as well as adding useful suggestions for alternative details. This emphasises how essential it is for working details to be carefully prepared and checked. Every part of a job must be considered to ensure that, as far as possible, all necessary site information is included, that details are practicable for the operatives, that they are suitable for their particular circumstances, and that they will be technically and visually satisfactory in performance. The preface to the first edition of Gunn's book is equally applicable to this: 'The author makes no claim to anything sensational in the matter of these notes. Some of the expedients are very old ones, some are possibly new, and these latter are not all of his own origination. He believes that every architect who strikes or avoids a "snag" ought to open the matter to his fellows. Quacks secrete, scientists publish.'

However, the opinions in these studies, unlike Gunn's book, are not those of one person only. They are the results of a great deal of discussion (and not a little argument) among a team of six. This team is headed by Cecil Handisyde, an architect in private practice with experience of research at BRS and of teaching; a frequent contributor to *The Architects' Journal* and author of various books related to building science and construction.

The other team members are:

Allan Hodgkinson, consulting engineer and member of the Kenneth Severn Group; also a frequent contributor to *The Architects' Journal* and a consultant editor for the *AJ Handbook of Building Structure*.

Douglas Robertson, quantity surveyor, principal of Surveyors' Collaborative and director of the Building Cost Information Service (BCIS) and the Building Maintenance Cost Information Service (BMCIS).

Philip Berry, chief supervisor, Yorke Rosenberg Mardall.

F. R. Leeman, senior site agent, John Laing Construction Ltd.

Leslie Fairweather, editor of *The Architects' Journal*.

When giving costs we have retained the data current when the details were originally published in *The Architects' Journal*. These data cover such things as comparative costs of damp-proof membranes (detail 1, page 1), and of tile hanging and timber cladding (detail 9, page 45). The principles of such comparisons will not have changed, but we advise readers to bear in mind increases caused by inflation since 1973-74.

1

Ground floor construction

General

There has been a gradual change from suspended to solid ground floor construction. Loading conditions, floor finish requirements, thermal insulation and other factors may all be significant, but cost is frequently an important reason for using solid construction.

For houses, schools and other buildings where floor loads are light, the main influence on comparative costs of suspended or solid ground floors is the depth of hardcore fill. This depends on how much topsoil is removed and, when a floor without changes in level is needed, on site levels. **1** shows that, for the specified examples of construction, a solid floor is likely to be cheaper in first cost than traditionally constructed timber floors, unless hardcore fill exceeds an average thickness of about 500 mm. Forms of suspended timber construction omitting site concreting would be cheaper than traditional suspended floors, and are claimed by TRADA* to be cheaper than solid floor construction.

While **1** indicates where it is more economical to choose solid or traditional suspended floors, the break-even point varies depending upon when all details are known. For example the specification may require timber to be treated with preservative or the suspended floor to have added thermal insulation. These are fairly obvious examples which may directly affect the cost comparison but other design decisions (eg position of concrete slab and height of sleeper walls) make this a complex problem. Five variables of some significance are covered under the following headings: Ground floor levels, Oversite excavation, Hardcore, Oversite damp-proof membranes, Oversite concrete.

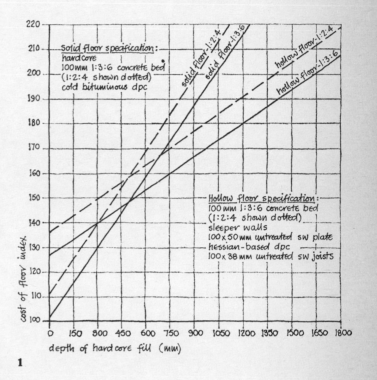

Solid floor specification:
hardcore
100mm 1:3:6 concrete bed
(1:2:4 shown dotted)
cold bituminous dpc

Hollow floor specification:
100 mm 1:3:6 concrete bed
(1:2:4 shown dotted)
sleeper walls
100 x 50 mm untreated sw plate
hessian-based dpc
100 x 38 mm untreated sw joists

cost of floor index

depth of hardcore fill (mm)

1

Ground floor levels

Suspended floors

In suspended ground floor construction, **2, 3**, the floor level in relation to foundations and site concrete affects overall job cost through its effect on wall height. The costs of excavation and hardcore are not directly influenced by floor level, but decisions on the level of oversite concrete will affect hardcore cost.

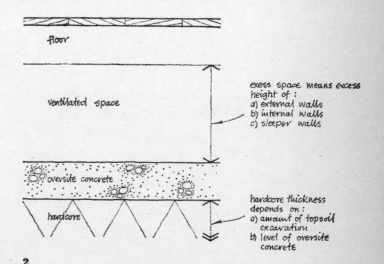

floor

ventilated space

oversite concrete

hardcore

excess space means excess height of:
a) external walls
b) internal walls
c) sleeper walls

hardcore thickness depends on:
a) amount of topsoil excavation
b) level of oversite concrete

2

* Timber Research and Development Association

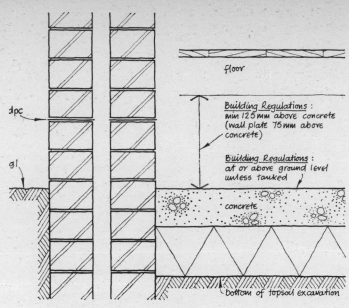

note: oversite concrete may be at level which allows the concrete to fill part of topsoil excavation space (this seldom applies with solid floor construction)

3

On sloping sites, stepping the oversite concrete, **4**, is more economical in hardcore than **5**, which keeps concrete at one level; note, however, that **5** may result in the top of site concrete falling below ground level which, without tanking precautions, would contravene Building Regulations.

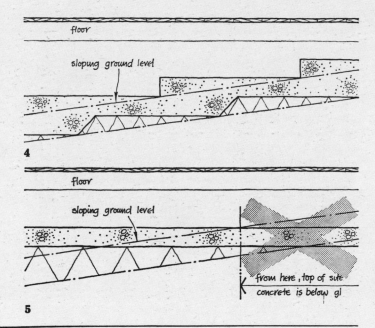

4

5

Solid floors

With solid ground floors, decisions about floor level not only affect wall heights but also directly influence thickness, and therefore cost, of hardcore (see **1**).

The level of oversite concrete damp-proof membrane (dpm) in relation to wall damp-proof course (dpc) affects damp exclusion details and costs (see 'Oversite damp-proof membranes').

On level sites the oversite concrete is usually positioned to provide a floor finish above ground level, **6**. The bottom of concrete is therefore at or above ground level. *All* topsoil excavation has to be replaced by hardcore and any raising of ground floor level means extra hardcore.

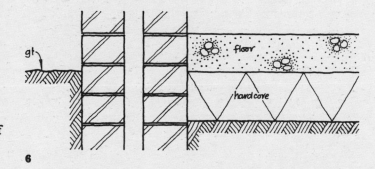

6

On sloping sites where the floor is maintained level throughout, depth of hardcore may become considerable, 7. Excessive thickness makes proper compaction difficult to ensure. Hardcore should be laid and compacted in layers of about 150 mm. If average thickness of hardcore is likely to be more than about 500 mm it is worth considering suspended floor construction or lowering the finished floor level and using vertical damp-course tanking, either of which may be cheaper than increased hardcore thickness.

With solid floors it may prove convenient if, by minor adjustment of levels, the oversite dpm lines through with wall dpc (see 'Oversite damp-proof membranes').

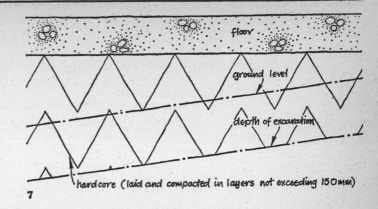

7

hardcore (laid and compacted in layers not exceeding 150mm)

Oversite excavation

The depth of oversite excavation affects hardcore cost and excavation cost but the implications of hasty office decisions to 'remove topsoil to a depth of x mm' are not always appreciated. Opinions about what constitutes 'topsoil' vary and neither textbooks nor the Building Regulations are very helpful. The Regulations require the site to be 'effectively cleared of turf and other vegetable matter'. Topsoil may vary from almost nil to a metre or more and it may have been cultivated to a considerable depth and contain deep rooted vegetation or have been undisturbed for centuries and have only turf growing on its top layer.

The architect may reconsider his decision after seeing the ground during excavation. This may mean an unwelcome increase in cost both in more excavation and in the resulting extra hardcore—one of the hard facts of life is that an *over* estimate of excavation seldom seems to occur! Site survey or trial hole information should therefore be sufficient for correct decisions to be made before completing design stage.

The amount of topsoil removal should be decided by:
1 Determining the *minimum* depth of excavation needed to remove *growing* vegetation, special allowance being made for isolated trees or other local conditions.
2 Checking whether this minimum requirement satisfies requirements of the proposed floor construction. This may involve deciding whether *any* hardcore is necessary, 8. The minimum removal depth may reach soil considered unsatisfactory for heavily loaded solid floors and further excavation may be required for that reason.
3 Considering whether additional excavation might be worthwhile to provide extra topsoil for site landscaping.

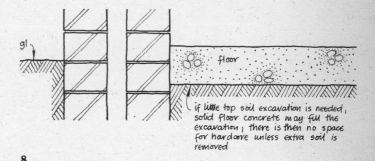

8

if little top soil excavation is needed, solid floor concrete may fill the excavation; there is then no space for hardcore unless extra soil is removed

If there is surplus topsoil on the site and it is scarce locally, the contractor should be invited to give a credit for its sale. With machine excavation, much of the total cost on small jobs is getting the machine to site, so additional excavation may show a cost benefit if topsoil is needed on the job or can be sold locally.

Where there is a considerable depth of poor strength material, soil consolidation might be a possible alternative. This is unlikely to be satisfactory on small sites, and should only be done elsewhere under expert control.

Hardcore

Is the function of hardcore always fully considered? In the past, especially when laid beneath solid floors, broken brick was universally used and was assumed to reduce rising damp from the soil penetrating into the site concrete. Now that Building Regulations 'deemed to satisfy' method (which uses a continuous dpm to solid floors) is widely used, hardcore as a means of damp prevention seems unnecessary.

Given good ground and dry weather, site concrete could be placed without any hardcore. In such conditions additional excavation to make room for hardcore is a waste of money. In wet weather, hardcore provides a working surface and where there is poor soil it can be rolled in, whereas soil alone would not accept a roller. An excess of hardcore is of no value and may well be a disadvantage as it is difficult to ensure good material and good compaction.

Hardcore has traditionally been specified as 'good clean brick broken to pass a 4in ring, or other approved material'. Nowadays this often produces a load of mixed rubbish containing anything from old plaster and bits of timber to large lumps of brick walling. This gets tipped into position when the architect is not on site and it becomes difficult to enforce a satisfactory result. The thicker the hardcore the more difficult it is to avoid cavities into which upper layer material may later subside, 9.

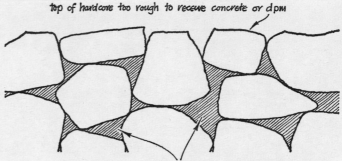

top of hardcore too rough to receive concrete or dpm

cavities resulting from use of large, thick hardcore

9

A moderate thickness, 100 to 150 mm after consolidation, of well graded stones, or the use of hoggin* as a fill material, is preferable to a thick poor fill. Hoggin is usually considerably dearer than hardcore. In Scotland, an alternative material is blaes (oil shale), but this must be well burnt, and should have less than 0·2 per cent concentration of sulphates.

The top finish to hardcore is important. If concrete is placed directly on it the top surface should be blinded with sand unless there is sufficient fine material to roll out to a surface into which cement grout from the concrete will not be lost. When the oversite dpm is designed to go beneath the concrete a fairly smooth base is required and nearly always a layer of rolled sand is necessary.

The Building Regulations require hardcore to be free from water-soluble sulphates or other deleterious matter in such quantities as to be liable to cause damage to any part of the floor. Top blinding material should also meet this requirement and for this reason it is seldom safe to use ashes.

Oversite damp-proof membranes

On almost all buildings with solid ground floors the Building Regulations 'deemed to satisfy' clauses require a continuous dpm. This is sometimes placed beneath the oversite concrete, sometimes as a sandwich between slab and screed and sometimes on top of the concrete when it is used as a combined dpm and floor finish adhesive, eg with timber finish on asphalt or pitchmastic or hot bitumen.

* Hoggin: a naturally occurring sand gravel mixture with a very small clay content; just sufficient to bind the material under the action of the roller

The floor dpm must be joined to wall dpcs. The implications of this and other factors upon the choice of position for the dpm are considered below.

A smooth base is needed to prevent damage to a thin sheet membrane, **10**. Rolled sand, at least 25 mm, is suitable but by no means always specified. Any joints in a sheet membrane need to be sealed, either by double folding or by lapping 150 mm and sealing with suitable adhesive.

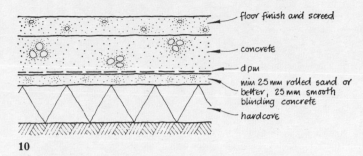

floor finish and screed
concrete
dpm
min 25mm rolled sand or better, 25mm smooth blinding concrete
hardcore

10

Considerable care is needed to avoid membrane damage while concrete is being placed. Damage may not be visible and is almost impossible to find or repair at a later date, so it is essential to use a tough impact-resisting material. Concrete cannot dry downward so time for adequate drying upward is essential before applying many floor finishes.

Where ground contains harmful sulphates a dpm beneath the concrete may give adequate protection and obviate the need to use sulphate-resisting cement for the concrete. Check that dpm will protect concrete from harmful sulphates. (It will only be effective if continuous, and will not protect against sulphate heave.) The additional cost of sulphate-resisting cement in a 100 mm slab of 1:2:4 mix would be about 6p/m² or 6 per cent of the cost of the slab.

If a lightweight concrete slab is used protection from ground moisture is essential if thermal insulation value is to be maintained. In such cases dpm must go beneath concrete.

A smooth base is needed to prevent damage if a thin sheet membrane is used. Even with in situ brushed material, a reasonably smooth concrete surface is advisable. Smooth surfaces are likely to increase the concrete cost by about 12 per cent above spade finishing, **11**.

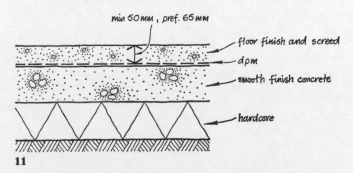

min 50mm, pref. 65mm
floor finish and screed
dpm
smooth finish concrete
hardcore

11

An advantage of brush-applied dpm materials is that they can be continued more easily as a vertical membrane up walls to link with the wall dpc (see **19** on page 23).

Care is needed to prevent dpm being damaged before or while laying floor screeding.
A sandwich membrane prevents satisfactory bonding between screed and slab and a thick screed becomes necessary. A 50 mm thickness should be considered absolute minimum (63 mm preferable), even though this

would be about 20 per cent dearer than a 35 mm screed. Chasing for pipes let into screed may damage the dpm although a thick screed encourages accommodation of small pipes. Pipes or ducts should be fixed before any screed is poured, rather than chasing out later.

John Weller of Bildeston, Ipswich wrote: 'I have specified for a small domestic extension a polythene membrane laid below the site concrete and over 25 mm rolled sand over hardcore. This is in accordance with your figure **10** and I believe to be satisfactory construction. The Suffolk Coastal District Council believes that this detail specification does not conform to the Building Regulations. I should appreciate your comment whether the detail as published has led to any adverse comment either in use or from other applications for Building Regulations.'

Philip Berry replied: 'We have had no experience of rejection of use of polythene under the site slab, though, except in one case, polythene has been laid on top of concrete blinding. Polythene alone is not acceptable under finishes such as wood block flooring or vinyl which are susceptible to water vapour (Regulation C5), but is satisfactory under vinyl asbestos or thermoplastic flooring. Regulation C3 (1) requires that a floor next to the ground shall prevent passage of moisture. Polythene would seem to comply. Regulation C3 (2) requires that a floor be so constructed as to prevent any part of the floor being adversely affected by moisture or vapour from the ground. So acceptability of polythene depends on the floor finish.'

The GLC commented: 'Even on rolled sand a sheet dpm should not be less than 1000 gauge. Double folding or welting of sheet dpms is difficult to execute—it jumps apart. Adhesive tape jointing is better.
'If there are sulphates in sufficient quantity in the soil, sulphate-resisting cement must always be used. The dpm might be punctured.
'While some brush-applied dpm materials do comply with the Building Regulations, they must always be subject to faulty workmanship.
'Pipes and ducts should always be fixed before screed is poured—chasing is not on.'

Wood finishes

The method illustrated in **12** is deemed to satisfy Building Regulations if the damp-proofing layer is asphalt or pitch-mastic not less than 12 mm thick *or* if it is hot soft bitumen or coal-tar pitch forming a continuous layer as adhesive to wood block flooring of not less than 16 mm thickness.

If asphalt or pitchmastic is used immediately beneath the floor finish it can be applied late in the job and be less liable to sitework damage. Also it is visible until the floor finish is laid.

Provided its thickness is not reduced below the minimum requirements a mastic dpm of nominal 12 mm can fill in roughness or make good minor variations of level in the site concrete. Normal screeding may then be unnecessary. Floor service pipes are completed before the dpm is laid so damage from them is less likely.

When using the thin, wood block adhesive method, it is virtually impossible to check that a 'continuous layer' has been achieved. There is therefore an element of risk, especially on damp sites. As this form of dpm is thin it must go on a smooth surface, so floor screeding is usually needed, with attendant risk of cracking. Mastic asphalt screeds are free of these risks.

Comparative costs of dpms are shown in table I.

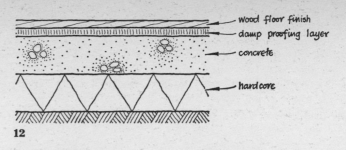

wood floor finish
damp proofing layer
concrete
hardcore

12

Table I Comparative cost of damp-proof membranes†

Damp-proof membrane	Cost index
0·13 mm polythene sheet	25
Two coats cold bitumen emulsion	85
Three coats cold bitumen emulsion	100
Two coats bituminous latex emulsion	135
3 mm hot soft bitumen	150
3 mm hot coal tar pitch	160
12 mm mastic asphalt BS 1097	400*
16 mm pitchmastic to BS 1450	430*
12 mm mastic asphalt BS 1418	530*
29 mm mastic asphalt BS 1097	640*
29 mm mastic asphalt BS 1418	895*

*If by the use of these thick materials the need for a 35 mm floor screed is eliminated, the saving would offset the tabulated comparative figures by a reduction of 200 points
† Costs as at October 1973

Oversite concrete

Design and specification of oversite concrete is not always based upon logical consideration of requirements.

English Building Regulations 'deemed to satisfy' description is for a minimum of 100 mm of oversite concrete of a mix not weaker than 50 kg cement/0·1 m³ fine aggregate/0·2 m³ coarse aggregate. In practice concrete seems to vary from 100 to 150 mm or more in thickness, sometimes plain but sometimes (usually in the better quality concrete) reinforced by varying amounts of steel and with a mix specification of anything from the Regulation minimum (equivalent to 1:3:6) up to 1:2:4 or better. The quality of any particular mix varies widely according to type of aggregate, water/cement ratio and general workmanship factors.

The price implications of variations in oversite concrete are shown in table II.

Table II Comparative cost of oversite concrete (100 mm thick plain concrete 1:3:6 is base index of 100)*

Concrete thickness	1:3:6 mix Plain	1:2:4 mix Plain	2·22 kg/m² mesh	5·55 kg/m² mesh
100 mm	100	105	160	215
125 mm	120	125	185	240
150 mm	145	150	210	265

NB: Quality, other than mix, assumed similar throughout; reinforcement assumed as single layer steel mesh
* Costs as at October 1973

On very poor soils site concrete should be designed either as a raft, taking wall or column as well as floor loads, or as a suspended slab carried on walls which transmit the load to foundations. Individually calculated slabs are also necessary for heavily loaded floors such as some factories, warehouses, floors carrying considerable wheeled loads or where other special considerations apply.

For a great many buildings actual loads on oversite concrete are small, frequently averaging less than 0·47 kN/m² and probably not exceeding 14·6 kN/m² over small areas where load is concentrated. In most cases of this kind site concrete is not calculated but is decided using 'balanced judgment'. Before making decisions the following questions might be considered:

1 Is *average* soil bearing capacity less than 24·4 kN/m²? If so, consider a designed raft or 'suspended' floor transmitting load to walls or frame.

2 Is *average* load likely to approach average soil capacity? This can occur with heavy loads and poor soil. Special measures may have to be taken (eg piling or soil stabilisation). In extreme cases the site may be unsuitable.

3 Will local loads over small areas approach *average* soil capacity? If so, slab must be adequate to spread the local load.

4 Is site on made-up ground? Consider reinforced slab, and measures necessary to isolate edges from main structure to allow for differential settlement. Consider how much settlement is acceptable.

5 Is hardcore more than about 150 mm thick? Consider reinforced slab or take special precautions to ensure proper quality and compaction of hardcore. The extra cost of a reinforced slab (see table II) is considerable and may seem too heavy an 'insurance'.

6 Is bearing capacity of soil liable to be affected by high water table? (Water table may often vary in different seasons and, with fissured clay, in different parts of the same site.) Use stronger slab than for similar soil in drier situation.

7 Is it worthwhile strengthening the oversite concrete to take some or all internal partitions or wall loads, thereby avoiding wall foundations?
See detail 4, page 16, 'Foundations to internal walls'.

Having assessed the general situation alternative solutions may be considered. Table III indicates types of slab likely to be reasonable for a variety of conditions.

A 1:2:4 mix is likely to have about twice the strength of a 1:3:6 mix, and as seen from table II the price difference is not great. The weaker mix is not advised except for light loads on stable soils (case (a) in table III).

Any slab which is reinforced should be 1:2:4 quality in order to provide reasonable protection to the steel.

The use of light reinforcement in thin slabs is primarily to tie the slab together and reduce risk of shrinkage cracks. In such cases the mesh should lie approximately in the centre of the slab. To be fixed easily, the lower half of the concrete would be placed, the mesh laid, followed immediately by upper concrete (ie prior to any initial set).

Designed reinforcement needs careful positioning. A single layer needs blocking up and when two layers are used the top one should be supported on reinforcement chairs.

In general it is probably better to have a poor slab on a good base rather than a good slab on a poor base. For this reason attention should be given especially to quality and compaction of hardcore (see 'Hardcore', page 4).

The requirements for quality of finish to the top of the oversite concrete, ie how level and how smooth, may be affected by:
1 Type of dpm, if on top of the concrete (see 'Oversite damp-proof membranes', page 4).
2 Type of floor finish if there is no intervening screed.

Table III Oversite concretes for domestic and other light-load conditions

Design conditions	Soil type	Hardcore thickness, mm	Concrete thickness, mm Unreinforced	Reinforced with mesh (kg/m²)
Natural ground	Stable (well graded sand or gravel)	0–100	100 (a)	100/2·2
	Normal (poorly graded sand, average clays)	0–100	125	100/2·2
	Unstable (organic soil, soft clay, peat)	100–150	Unsuitable	125/5·5*
Fill or made-up ground	Compacted sand or gravel	Not needed	Unsuitable	125/2·2*
	Compacted average soils	0–100	Unsuitable	150/5·5*
Water table within 600 mm of surface	Stable	150	125	100/2·2
	Normal	150	150	125/2·2
	Unstable	150	150	125/5·5*

NB: With soft underlying strata and in mining subsidence areas a reinforced raft and structural separation will be necessary
*In these cases it may be necessary to treat the slab as suspended, with bearings on walls; hardcore thickness may be reduced or, if convenient, hardcore may be omitted and the soil covered with blinding concrete prior to laying the slab

2

Strip foundations to external walls

General

For small, single-storey buildings with spans up to about
10 m or buildings with domestic type spans and heights up
to three storeys, the choice of strip type footings is less
obvious than it used to be. On clay soils, short bored piles
may be preferable, while for light loading on bad ground,
raft foundations are becoming more frequent (see detail 3,
page 11). In spite of this, strip footings remain the most usual.

Old text books put great emphasis upon foundation *width*
but said little about depth below ground. The 1972 Building
Regulations allow quite narrow foundations for small
building loads on moderate ground such as sandy clay
(Class IV, table to Regulation D7), while recognition of the
dangers of clay soil shrinkage has resulted in more emphasis
on the need for depth.* Simultaneously there has been the
change from hand to machine excavation, with its speed,
ease of digging deep and narrow trenches and preference for
digging in uninterrupted straight lines. At the same time
the balance of costs has changed to make economy in labour
relatively more attractive than economy in some materials.

In spite of these changes, designs for strip foundations and
walls up to ground level, even if modified to some extent,
still seem to cling to the traditional form. In the following
examples the implications upon cost and other aspects are
examined for two designs of strip foundation.

Examples

A small building is assumed to have external wall loading of
approximately 33 kN/m run of wall.

Some old books would have suggested a foundation width
of as much as twice the wall plus 6in on either side, ie about
2ft 10in (865 mm) for an 11in wall.

Building Regulations 'deemed to satisfy' requirements would
be met by a foundation width of 400 mm on stiff clay or
450 mm width on firm clay. On poorer soils, 'deemed to
satisfy' requirements do not allow for loadings of more than
30 kN/m run and even for that loading require foundation
widths from 600 mm to 850 mm, according to soil
conditions. For very poor soil, raft type foundations have
always been regarded as necessary.

On clay soils the depth from ground level to bottom of
foundation should be about 1 m but greater depth may be
needed in some cases,* eg where nearby trees may cause
excessive drying of the clay in summer (see BRS Digest 67,
HMSO).

In the examples which follow, a depth of 1 m and width of
450 mm has been assumed to satisfy the requirements.

* The exceptional drought during 1976 caused considerable damage to buildings
on clay soils.

Concrete strip footing with brick wall

Trench concrete filled up to oversite excavation level

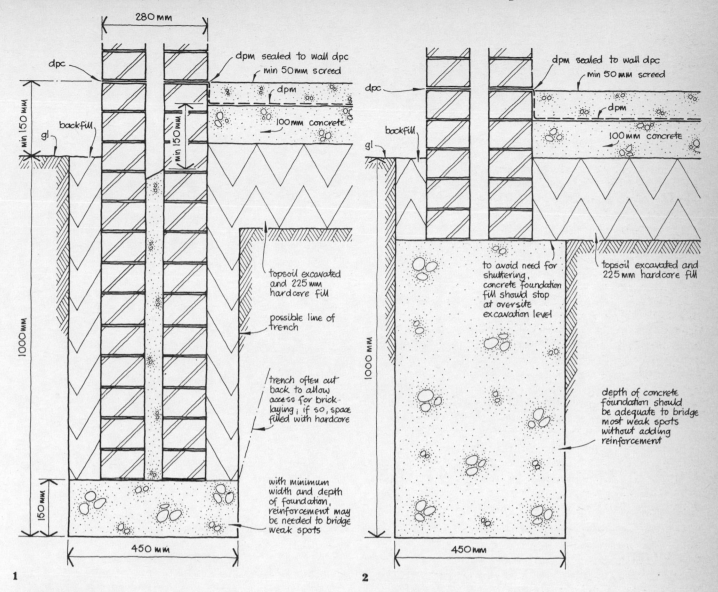

1

2

Process 1 involves:
Excavation.
Some carting away—rather less than in 2.
Concrete.
Brickwork—at low level and in inconvenient trench.
Cavity grouting.
Some backfill—which has been retained on site, causing obstruction.
Some hardcore fill.

Process 2 involves:
Excavation.
Carting away—almost all material removed, leaving site clear.
Concrete.
Brickwork—but only at relatively easy working position.
Small topsoil backfill.

Comparison of 1 and 2
In **1** the process will be slower and the open trench more vulnerable to bad weather for longer than in **2**. It is easier to run pipes through walling with **1** than with **2**. In both **1** and **2**, placing the dpm below the concrete would prevent grout seeping into the hardcore, but in this position the dpc itself might be damaged before or while placing the concrete. Blinding is essential if dpc is below concrete.

Comparative costs
A true cost comparison of foundation **1** with foundation **2** is based not only on the substitution of concrete for brick but also on economies in labour content of the building procedures and processes employed. Benefits from speed or ease of construction or less risk of damage are not always clearly shown by measurements in bills of quantities; nor may the contractors' estimates make a sufficient study of the drawings to understand any economies of production incorporated in the design.

Table I, presented as index ranges, shows probable cost relationships for cases **1** and **2**. These are based upon prices of items *without* making allowances for non-measurable production savings on site. Even on this basis, although the cost ranges of foundations **1** and **2** overlap, foundation **2** should be generally cheaper.

The GLC made these points:
'1 Figures indicate about 80 mm backfill externally. This is a difficult width to backfill.
2 The trench excavation would need to be wider to build brickwork below ground level.
3 The cavity grouting drainage fillet should preferably be above the ground line to drain the cavity.
4 Process 2 is preferred to process 1 and is cheaper. The cavity grouting and drainage fillet have been omitted. There are advantages in having the dpm below the concrete. With dpm beneath the screed, cracking of the screed at its junction with the wall is known to occur.'

Cecil Handisyde replied:
'1 Agreed this would be significant for the depth in **1** but not in **2**.
2 **1** indicates the probable need to widen the trench (shown on the inside). If more width is considered necessary the cost will increase, and this should be considered in comparison with process 2.
3 Agreed this is desirable. The question might then arise as to whether the floor structure must be raised in order to maintain the floor dpm 150 mm above the bottom of the cavity. This is not stated as a requirement under Building Regulation C5(c) and should not be necessary if the floor dpm is correctly joined to the wall dpc.
4 It is doubtful whether cavity grouting is necessary for the small depth if hardcore consolidation is done carefully to avoid damage to the walling. The position of the dpm is debatable: if placed beneath the concrete it is more liable to damage during construction, and a much longer time must be allowed for the drying out of thick concrete before laying most types of floor finish.'

Table I Cost relationships for foundation types A and B*

Foundation type	Concrete mix 1-3-6	Concrete mix 1-2-4
	100-122	101-124
	90-110	93-114

Figures give index ranges calculated on prices at first quarter 1971 and based on designs A and B.

* Costs as at October 1973

Materials
Brickwork has been taken as local common bricks in 1:3 cement/sand mortar.

Table I shows values for two concrete mixes. Strength of concrete may vary very considerably depending upon water content and grading of aggregate. In many cases a 1:3:6 mix should be adequate.

Walling might, in some cases, be of suitable quality concrete blocks rather than brick.

In clay soils, sulphates may be present in sufficient quantity to require higher quality concrete and brickwork.

Check list

Design
Assuming it has been decided to use strip footings:

From loading calculations and site survey information on soil, determine minimum overall depth and width of foundation (Building Regulations, Regulation D7).

Consider cost and other factors and decide between concrete footing with masonry walling and deep concrete trench.

Check service entry requirements compatible with foundation.

Decide positions for any vertical stepping of foundations on sloping sites.

Specification
Describe materials. Consider need to specify special precautions in high sulphate soils. Describe disposal of surplus excavation.

Make clear contractor responsibility for weather damage, water level conditions or other hazards.

Supervision
Check setting out. Check excavation dimensions.

Check soil is *all* as expected, or when necessary agree action for weak spots etc.

Immediately before concreting, check trench soil conditions. Also confirm service entry provisions.

Check quality of materials, and for thin concrete footings, check thickness as laid.

Check overlaps at changes in levels (Regulation D7 (e)).

Check materials and adequacy of compaction of backfill.

3

Raft foundations for small buildings

When to use raft foundations

To engineers, the term *raft* implies a stiffened slab
foundation, used instead of heavily loaded pad or strip
foundations which would, in any case, cover a considerable
part of the site. For small buildings, a stiffened slab would
be uneconomical, and the type of high-level foundation used
for them may be better described as a flexible strip footing
at ground level. It is this type of foundation which is
considered here.

Traditionally, rafts for small buildings were used only where
poor soil conditions made them the only feasible type of
foundation. An extension of their use has been in mining
areas. More recently they have been used for small
buildings on normal soils. There may be a case for more
general use of this type of foundation.

Advantages and disadvantages

These, considered at early design stage, should help to
decide whether detailed investigation is worthwhile. Cost
comparisons between raft and other types of foundation are
only feasible when related to specific cases but some
influencing factors are mentioned. The edge treatment of a
raft provides the main problems of structural design,
building details and visual effect, **1** to **4**.

Advantages
1 Simple machine excavation without trenching.
2 Absence of foundation trenches facilitates movement of
men and materials.
3 Excavation less liable than trenches to become
waterlogged or damaged in bad weather.
4 Less interference with sub-soil water movements.
5 May eliminate need for awkward below-ground walling by
bricklayers.
6 Probably quicker than alternatives of strip or short pile
foundations.
7 In poor sites, they avoid penetrating poor bearing
materials just below the surface.

Disadvantages
1 May not be adequate for some loading and soil
conditions.
2 Ducts or pipe chases in the floor present problems.
3 Precautions usually need to be taken against drying
shrinkage or frost heaving of ground beneath the raft
perimeter.
4 Unequal load distribution, eg piers, may cause problems.
5 Rafts are seldom worth considering unless the site is
substantially level.

6 Many strip foundations for small buildings are decided by reference to Building Regulations with a minimum of calculation. Raft foundation design is less generally understood. In the absence of experience some offices may need the help of a consultant.

7 The quality of material beneath the raft, of the raft concrete, and the correct positioning of its reinforcement, are more important than in strip foundations. Adequate supervision on small jobs at a distance may be difficult to ensure.

8 Greater need to avoid excessive cold bridging owing to concrete slab continuing to outside.

Edge of raft detail

In determining the type of edge treatment for rafts the following points should be considered:

1 Provision of reasonable support for perimeter wall loads.
2 Prevention of weather effect causing either frost heave or drying shrinkage of ground beneath the edge of the raft.
3 Simple and efficient damp-proofing.
4 Accommodation of minor variations in ground levels.
5 Appearance.
6 Permanence of satisfactory support conditions.
7 Protection of steel and durability of reinforced concrete.

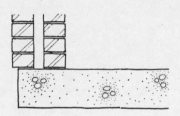

Reasonable support of perimeter wall loads
1 is suitable only for light loads. Load is eccentric, and heavy loads produce deflection and require a thicker slab and heavier reinforcement.

1

2 is different from 1 in that isolated pier loads can be spread along the edge of the slab. Loses advantage of single thickness slab and is unsuitable for mining areas, which require single thickness slab laid on level bed of sand and polythene sheet.

2

Compared to 1 and 2, 3 provides better spread of load and allows a uniform thinner slab to be used.

3

4 loses the advantage of uniform slab thickness but facilitates placing of mesh reinforcement and spreading of isolated pier loads along edge of slab. Not suitable for mining areas.

4

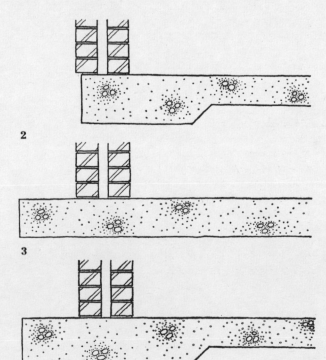

Protection against weather causing frost heave or drying shrinkage beneath the edge of the raft

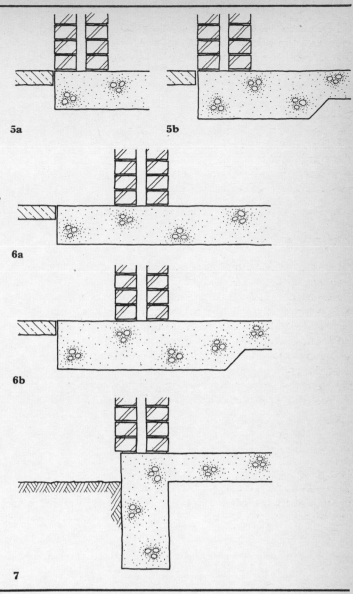

Protection from frost or drying must be in width outside of wall provided by paving, **5a**, or in combination of width and depth under the wall, **5b**.

In **6**, protection, as in **5**, is required. Without the paved area, the projecting raft slab could be damaged by lifting under frost action, or its toe may lose support by drying shrinkage. Paving should be minimum 600 mm wide slabs.

7 is satisfactory for weathering if depth of toe is 500 mm in well drained cohesionless soil, or 1000 mm in other soils. This method loses some of the advantages of a raft and almost becomes a strip footing. Is unsatisfactory in mining areas.

Simple and efficient damp-proofing

Projecting slab or paving collects rain. Cavity stops at top of raft. Damp-proofing depends upon fully efficient inside vertical membrane which is very difficult to achieve. Sloping the top of the outside concrete away from the wall gives only slight improvement. A better detail than **a** and **b** is shown in **c**, but unless top of raft is kept 150 mm above ground or paving it requires the extra dpc. Also dpc in **c** would be vulnerable to damage during cleaning out of the cavity, and is better resting against a solid backing.

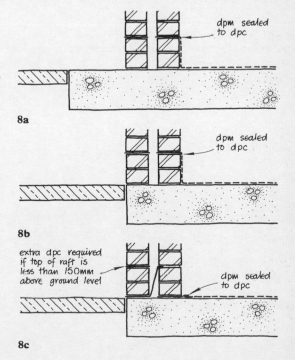

9 is satisfactory for damp-proofing, and for loading and weather protection. Placing of mesh reinforcement is easy. Loses advantage of simple, single-thickness slab.

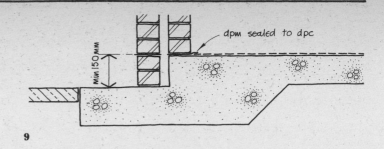

9

This detail, **10**, is sometimes shown as an alternative to **9** but is less satisfactory for damp-proofing.

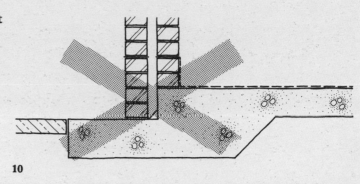

10

Accommodation of variations in ground levels

Raft construction of the type being considered here is normally considered only for 'level' sites. Minor variations in ground level are probably best dealt with by local adjustment of ground at the edge of the projecting paving, **11** (dpm to floor in **11**, **12**, **13**, **14** as **9**).

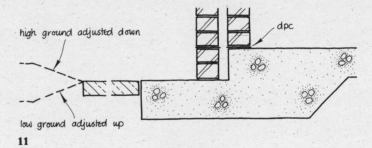

11

A deep downturn edge to the raft can accommodate ground-level variations and meets weather protection and dpc requirements, but it really reverts to being a deep strip footing and loses the advantages of a true raft, **12**.

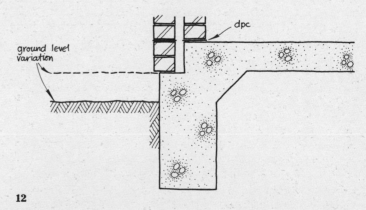

12

Appearance

Edge protection and the projection of the raft itself prevent normal cultivation immediately adjacent to a building, though some form of raised growing trough can be provided if care is taken to prevent damp penetration above the main wall dpc, **13**.

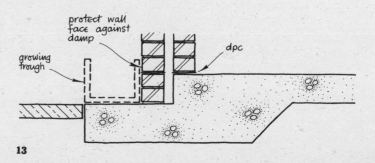

13

In **9** and **11**, an exposed strip of raft concrete meets the outer paving. If this is visually unacceptable, the concrete can be covered with paving, **14**, but this will lower the top of internal slab level in relation to outside ground. This may be acceptable but needs consideration, especially in relation to its effect on dpc levels and upon the *effective* depth of wall cavity below inner wall dpc level both of which must be at least 150 mm (Building Regulations C7 and C8).

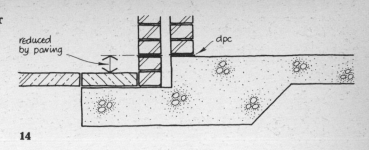

14

Maintenance

Protection against the effect of weather upon soil beneath the edge of the concrete raft must be preserved. Where paving forms a useful path system, the risk of alteration is probably small. Where the paving is not serving a useful purpose, its permanence is less certain. Ardent gardening house-owners probably provide the greatest risk. To ensure against removal, consider using in situ concrete paving.

Protection of steel and durability of concrete
Where exposed around the perimeter, the concrete must be of good quality and provide top or side cover to steel of at least 50 mm. Bottom cover to steel should not be less than 40 mm.

Cost aspects of rafts

Although detailed cost comparisons can be made only in specific cases, raft foundations may provide economical solutions, especially when moderately deep substructures would otherwise be required. An economic case can be made, particularly for designs which do not use a projecting slab, and, where structurally acceptable, it is likely to be more economic to thicken the slab than to project it beyond the external face of the walling. The following notes give some indication of when rafts may be used:

1 As an alternative to deep footings.
2 When high water table would complicate trench excavations.
3 Where perimeter wall loads are very light, eg timber frame walls, a simple raft may cost less.
5 Unlikely to be satisfactory or economic on sloping sites.
6 Unlikely to be satisfactory or economic when loading is very uneven, eg heavy pier loads.
7 Unlikely to be economic when ground conditions and wall loads permit shallow strip footings.

Structural design

Simple design of small raft foundations, including ground slabs, is given in *AJ Handbook of Building Structure* Information sheet Foundations 5, page 146 (The Architectural Press, 1974).

David White commented: 'It is rather difficult to persuade local authorities on details such as those illustrated in **1** and **5a** (Regulation D3(b)). They insist that the edge of the beam is thickened down below the ground even on subsidence sites. Can you help in supplying references?'

Allan Hodgkinson replied: 'There are no formal references as such because so much depends upon local site conditions and on the judgment of the local inspectors responsible for enforcing the Regulations. There are many variations in site

conditions, and Building Regulations, by their very nature, can deal only with the general rather than with the particular. The problem is discussed fairly fully in CP 2004: 1972, pages 31 and 32,* but the final decision must depend on local experience and knowledge. *Everyday Details* can deal only with acceptable forms of construction for most situations, but particular local conditions may call for the use of one rather than another of the details.'

Cecil Handisyde replied: 'The details include several references to the need to ensure that edge treatment is suitable, eg page 13. It is likely that the treatment in **1** would be acceptable only for very light edge loading and on favourable soils. Protection by external paving, **5a**, should considerably extend the acceptability of the simple method shown in **1**, at least on soils where seasonal drying is a main consideration.'

* Available from British Standards Institution, 2 Park Street, London W.1

4

Foundations to internal walls

Choice of foundation

Foundations for internal loadbearing walls above two-storey height are usually calculated. Where there are suspended floors, lightweight partitions may be carried off the floor. Non-loadbearing partitions are normally carried on oversite concrete in solid floor construction. Besides such cases, there are many internal walls carrying light or medium loads, for which foundations are determined by judgment rather than calculation.

Before considering possible alternatives, the following general points should be noted:

1 Except for some types of non-loadbearing partitions, internal walls are usually bonded to external walls. The possibility of differential settlement of internal and external walling may be more important than minor movement of the internal walls above. Movement which would not be structurally serious, nor visually significant on exposed brickwork, could cause unacceptable cracking of plaster finishes near external wall junctions.

2 Walls, although themselves supported adequately on concrete sub-floors, may cause that concrete to crack and affect floor finishes.

3 Seasonal effects, such as frost or drying-out, which may determine the depth of external wall foundations are less important to internal foundations.

4 Designs which are apparently logical do not always satisfy local Building Inspectors who are apt to have strong views about foundation requirements. It can be very inconvenient if this becomes apparent only when work is in progress. Prior agreement should be reached if possible.

5 When in doubt choose a 'poor' (small spread) foundation on good ground rather than a 'good' (wide spread) foundation on poor ground, 1.

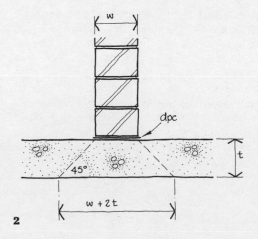

1

Types of foundation

Wall direct on unreinforced oversite concrete on hardcore
2 eliminates cost of foundation and site nuisance of excavated trenches.

If wall is to carry any superstructure, this means ground slab, on which it rests, may have to be placed earlier than would otherwise be desirable. But 2 is usually suitable only for non-loadbearing partitions.

However, if hardcore is not thick or is well compacted, and soil is as good as well compacted sand or gravel, 2 may be satisfactory for light loads—up to about 15 kN/m run depending upon type of walling, finish, and acceptability of some risk of cracks near junctions to external walls.

If, as is common practice, an internal wall dpc is at oversite concrete level, it may *not* be at the same level as the external wall dpc. It this is so, the wall junction detail should include a vertical dpc to ensure continuity of protection.

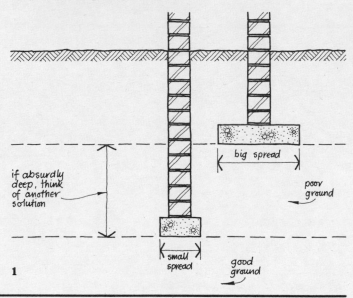

2

Wall on unreinforced concrete, thickened to depth of hardcore

3ab is similar to **2** but prevents settlement due to poor hardcore. Where thickened base is in excavated soil, the extra thickness of concrete gives additional strength and allows more spreading of the load.

3 is better than **2** for light-load walls but still has differential movement risk.

Depending on type of hardcore, concrete may be thickened in a more convenient shape, as **3b**, avoiding the need to use vertical formwork.

2 and **3ab** show maximum spread for unreinforced concrete where w + 2t equals spread, providing load is not greater than soil-bearing capacity.

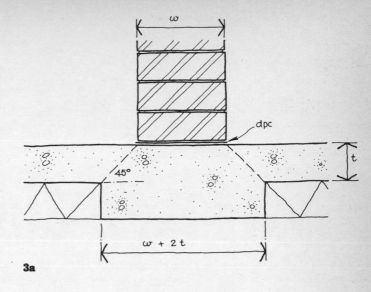

3a

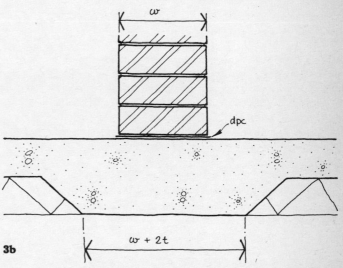

3b

Brick or block strip footing foundation

In **4abc** strip footings are carried down to good bearing soil but not to depth necessary for external walls exposed to frost or drying conditions. Near the perimeter, where the internal wall may be exposed, it should be dropped to full external wall depth, **4a**.

Excavated site trenches cause obstruction.

The foundation is formed at same time as external wall foundations. Hardcore and oversite concrete may be placed at any convenient time.

4 is suitable for loadbearing walls. Base size to follow tables in Building Regulation D7.

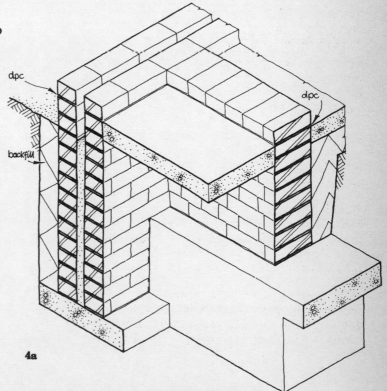

4a

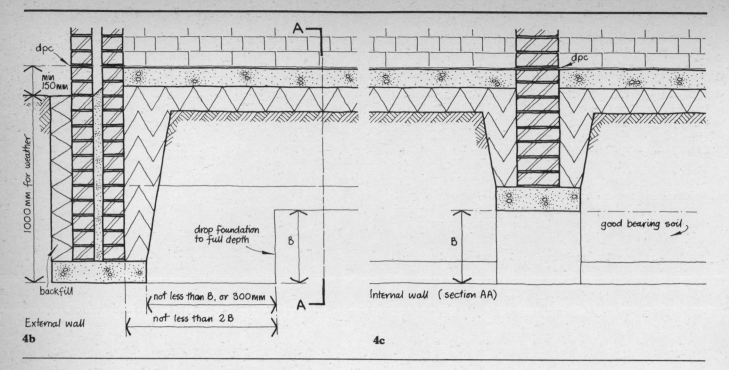

dpc

min 150mm

1000 mm for weather

backfill

drop foundation to full depth

B

not less than B, or 300mm

not less than 2B

A

A

External wall

4b

dpc

B

good bearing soil

Internal wall (section AA)

4c

Concrete strip footing foundation

5abc is similar to **4** but has narrow concrete-filled trench instead of walling down to concrete base. Trench can be excavated by machine, avoiding awkward low-level brick or block laying. (See also detail 2, page 8, 'Strip foundations to external walls'.)

In **5**, unlike **4**, it is essential to provide in advance for any below-ground services.

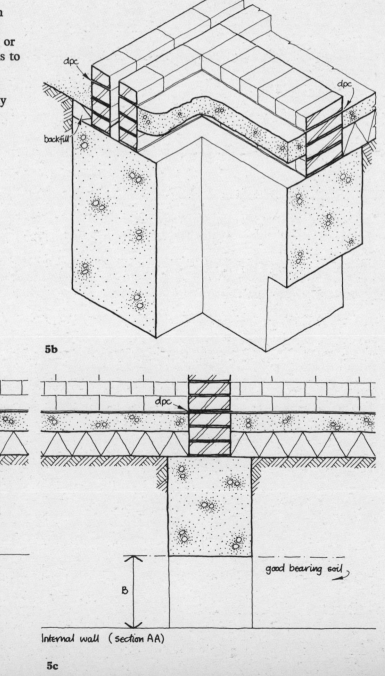

dpc

backfill

dpc

5b

dpc

min 150mm

1000 mm for weather

backfill

drop foundation to full depth

B

not less than B, or 300 mm

A

A

External wall

5a

dpc

B

good bearing soil

Internal wall (section AA)

5c

Reinforced concrete as raft to internal walls

This is used, **6ab**, where there is a raft or high-level strip footing to external walls.

A similar support for internal walls may be used with strip footing foundations to external walls if soil conditions are good and if internal wall loads are not very heavy. Tables I and II give examples of required concrete thickness and reinforcement for two types of soil conditions and various loadings.

6ab avoids the nuisance of internal trenches.

Site concrete must be placed to suit wall building programme.

The bottom steel is assumed to be carrying the load but concrete may crack along the outer limits of that reinforcement. For this reason, a light reinforcement at high level over the whole floor is advised (2·2 kg/m²).

Cover to steel should not be less than 40 mm, so oversite concrete cannot be less than 125 mm, as shown in **6**.

As an alternative to thickening the whole slab, concrete may be thickened locally under the slab, **7**, to width of w + 2t (see **3**).

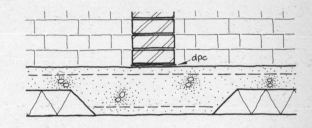

external wall   internal wall

6a   **6b**

7

Table I Concrete thickness and reinforcement required for oversite slab to carry internal walls on 27·5 kN/m² soil-bearing capacity

| Wall load | Soil-bearing capacity 27·5 kN/m² | | |
| | Min width of steel mesh[1] | Concrete thickness | Mesh weight |
kN/m run	mm	mm	kg/m²
15	800	125	2·22
20	800	125	2·22
25	900	125 150	3·02 or 2·22
30	1100	125 150	3·95 or 3·02
35	1300	125 150	6·16 or 3·95
40	1450	150	6·16
45	1600	175	6·16

1 Mesh is in bottom of slab with 40 mm cover. Sheet sizes 4·8 × 2·4 m can be cut economically to widths of 800, 1200 or 1600 mm

Table II Concrete thickness and reinforcement required for oversite slab to carry internal walls on 55 kN/m² soil-bearing capacity

| Wall load | Soil-bearing capacity 55 kN/m² | | |
| | Min width of steel mesh[1] | Concrete thickness | Mesh weight |
kN/m run	mm	mm	kg/m²
15	800	125	2·22
20	800	125	2·22
25	800	125	2·22
30	800	125	2·22
35	800	125 150	3·02 or 2·22
40	800	125 150	3·95 or 3·02
45	820	150	3·95

1 Mesh is in bottom of slab with 40 mm cover. Sheet sizes 4·8 m × 2·4 m can be cut economically to widths of 800, 1200 or 1600 mm

Cost comparisons

Table III, expressed as an index, compares the cost ranges for strip and concrete-filled narrow trench foundations to internal walls.

The cost comparison is based upon an 8 m run of one brick thick internal walling measured up to dpc level where the bottom of the external wall foundation is 1000 mm below ground level.

Table IV indicates cost relationships between strip or raft foundations for internal walls.

The cost comparison is based upon an 8 m run of one brick thick internal walling with solid concrete floor 6 m either side (but ignoring external walls).

Table III Index of foundation costs*

Description	Index ranges
Strip foundations carried down to good bearing soil with additional concrete at abutments with external wall foundations	100–120
Strip foundations at the level of external wall foundations for full length	190–230
Concrete-filled narrow trench foundations carried down to good bearing soil with additional concrete at abutments with external wall foundations	85–105
Concrete-filled narrow trench foundation at the level of external wall foundations for full length	120–150

*Costs as at January 1974

Table IV Cost relationship between strip and raft foundations*

Description	Index ranges
Concrete floor and strip foundation carried down to good bearing soil with additional concrete at abutments with external wall foundations	100–120
Concrete floor and concrete-filled narrow trench foundations carried down to good bearing soil with additional concrete at abutments with external wall foundations	95–120
Raft 125 mm thick over full floor area, for wall load of 30 kN/m run with soil loading 27·5 kN/m²	130–160
Raft 100 mm thick with additional concrete and reinforcement below internal walls, loading as above	125–150

* Costs as at January 1974

5

Masonry walls: dpc at base of external walls

External wall dpc

Although the change from solid to cavity walling, and from suspended to solid ground floors, is not recent, the implications of the change on dpc detailing are not always fully considered, as damp-proofing failures occur even on new buildings. Appearance also needs more attention.

Level of dpc at the external face of wall

A drawing showing a wall section at one position or a general instruction to keep the dpc 150 mm above adjacent ground is not really adequate. When working at dpc level, the workman does not always know where the final ground or paving levels will be—even the architect is not always sure.

Building Regulations require the dpc to be a *minimum* of 150 mm above ground level in the immediate vicinity. This may not be sufficient, since the wall immediately above the dpc may be damaged by splashing, and it is seldom a safe height above flower beds where earth often piles up.

Paving levels quite often seem to rise too close to the dpc, perhaps owing to late adjustments. The expected clearance of 150 mm, or more, disappears all too easily on sloping sites unless considerable care is taken with stepping the dpc.

Appearance of dpc at external wall face

Even the thinnest dpc material, if properly laid with mortar below and above, results in a thicker than normal joint. This cannot be avoided but, where the effect is considered important, the use of a thin damp-proofing material helps.

On sloping sites, the dpc is usually stepped at intervals with a vertical link. This thick vertical joint can be very unsightly. Travelling horizontally, the thickened dpc joint will change to a normal thin joint at the point where the dpc bends vertically down. So normal course lines are interrupted. Big vertical steps become particularly obtrusive.

Subject to site level requirements, it is worth trying to position the vertical steps where they will be least noticeable, eg behind planting or at internal corners, **1**, behind rain water pipes (if the positions of these can be accurately located in time and if pipe fixings will not be driven into the dpc) **2**.

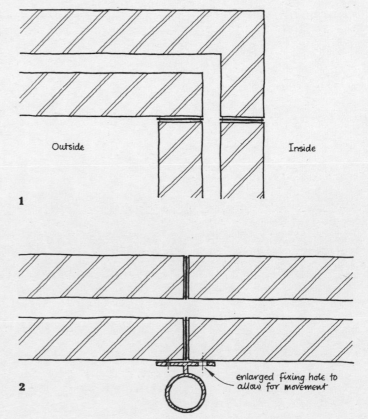

Outside

Inside

1

2

enlarged fixing hole to allow for movement

For the sake of appearance, the wall dpc is sometimes kept back from the wall-face and the joint pointed in mortar. Whether the damp 'bridge' which results is important depends upon whether the wall is of solid or cavity construction and, if cavity, whether the external material will be damaged if damp rises to it. A thick pointed joint is rather liable to deteriorate, especially if any wall movement occurs along the plane of the dpc, **3**.

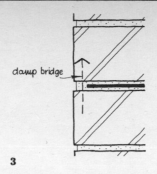

3

External dpc with rendered walls

Rendering should stop above the dpc level. Some published details recommend a projecting dpc, **4**. The turn down optimistically assumed on drawings is unlikely to be achieved with most materials. If it projects flat, **5**, it forms a ledge for water just where that is most harmful.

The dpc should always come to the edge of a rendered wall, but not beyond.

Opinions differ about the finish at the bottom of the rendering. With a fairly absorbent type of material, water run-off is usually minimal. With dense rendering and an exposed position, a 'throw-clear' detail may be advisable, **6**. For this, a bellmouth shape is commonly used but is rather easily damaged, especially if formed solely during the finish-coat of rendering. Where this detail is chosen, the shaping should be partially formed in the scratch coat of the rendering, or shaped with expanded metal lathing down from the bottom two courses of brickwork.

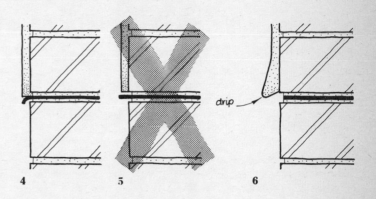

4   **5**   **6**

Dpc level at inside of external wall

With solid walls, it is inconvenient to have differing inside and outside levels. Bonding is interrupted and some dpc materials are difficult to bend satisfactorily. The problem can become very complicated where the line of the dpc must also vary to suit ground levels, **7**.

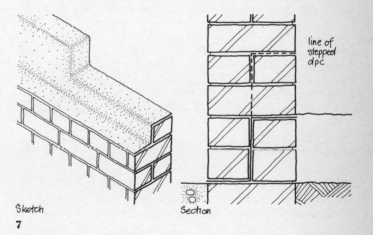

Sketch

7

Section

With cavity construction, inside and outside dpc levels can readily be different but the top of the dpc joint for *both* leaves should relate to the requirements of walling above, ie avoidance of cut courses at window openings and suitable coursing for floor support, **8**.

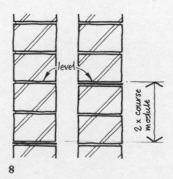

8

Suspended floors, minimum air space

With suspended ground floors, the wall dpc usually comes safely beneath the floor timbers, although there can be problems if underfloor ventilated space is reduced to the minimum permitted by the Building Regulations (ie 125 mm) for reasons of economy. With minimum 125 mm between oversite concrete and underside of joists, and with top of concrete almost at ground level, the wall dpc (150 mm above ground) may be at or above bottom of joists. So joists *must* be kept clear of wall, **9a** (or **9b** where joists run parallel to wall). Satisfactory positioning of airbricks is also difficult. In **9c**, airbricks are likely to be blocked by earth (unless paving surfaces are specified, and actually laid as shown on the architect's drawing). The airbrick in **9c** could be raised above the dpc, but this is less satisfactory with joists parallel to the wall, **9d**.

With solid ground floors, wall dpc and floor dpm must be linked to provide an unbroken moisture barrier. A vertical link is often needed for this (see **12, 14**).

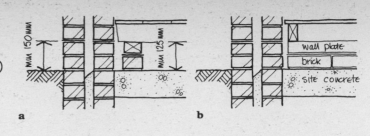
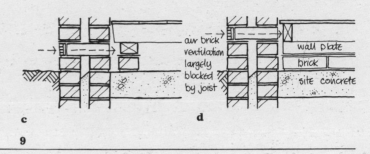

9

Dpc related to cavity

Where cavities are unfilled and extend down to foundation level, mortar droppings are no problem.

Where cavity grouting is required, it should finish at least 150 mm below *both* dpcs. If there is any doubt about proper clearance of mortar droppings from the bottom of the cavity, the 150 mm may not be sufficient, **10**.

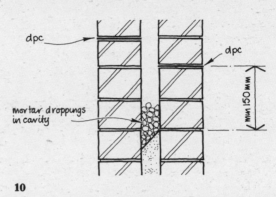

10

High level ground outside

Where a site slopes but ground floor level is constant, it is very easy to fail to notice that the inner wall dpc, although above the bottom of the cavity, is not above a level to which the cavity may fill with water, **11**.

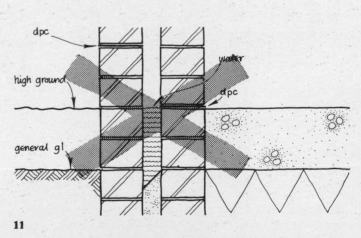

11

A somewhat similar risk arises when oversite dpm is at or near ground level, even though the wall dpcs are high enough. The vertical dpm on the inside of the walling is then subject to a more serious water condition than normal and needs to be treated as tanking rather than as a barrier to relatively minor rising dampness, **12**.

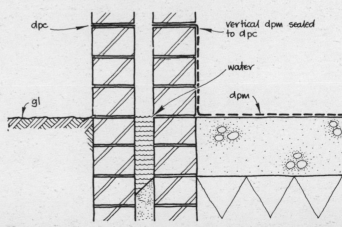

12

Linking wall dpc to floor dpm

Satisfactory continuity depends a great deal upon careful workmanship. The method to use depends on:
1 relative levels of wall and floor dpcs
2 relative times at which they can be laid
3 nature of damp-proofing material.

A common weakness is for the wall dpc to stop short of the inner wall face, **13**. This should be avoided in all cases except where the floor membrane can be run in to lap the wall dpc during wall building.

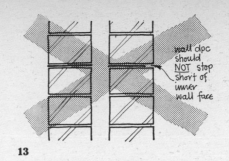

wall dpc should NOT stop short of inner wall face

13

Floor dpm

Floor membrane beneath oversite concrete

Floor membrane, usually of thin sheet material, is usually at a lower level than wall dpc. A vertical link is essential.

If oversite concrete is laid when walls reach dpc level, the floor membrane can be turned up and into the wall, lapping with the wall dpc, **14**. Care is needed to prevent damage while concreting and during subsequent site works. Damage may not be visible once floor concrete is placed.

If site concrete is not laid at wall dpc stage, a similar treatment with the floor membrane tucked into an open joint is possible but less easy to achieve satisfactorily.

An alternative, **15**, is to stop the turned up dpm at top of site concrete and form the vertical link as a separate operation—as late as possible to avoid site work damage. In this case, the vertical link would be a fluid dpm. It should pass above the wall dpc level and return on to the top of the oversite concrete with a generous application of material at the wall/floor joint.

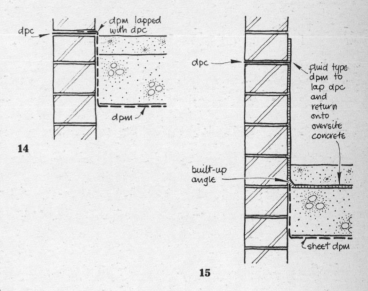

dpc — dpm lapped with dpc

dpm

14

dpc — fluid type dpm to lap dpc and return onto oversite concrete

built-up angle

sheet dpm

15

Floor membrane as sandwich between oversite concrete and screed

In this case, the floor membrane may be either a sheet material, or a fluid type, but the laying of either is not done until just before screeding of the floor.
Any vertical link dpm is easily seen and is not exposed to risk of site damage for long.

If the floor membrane is a flexible sheet material, it may be continued up the wall to pass beyond the dpc course, **16**.

Or a fluid type wall dpm may be applied to the wall and turned round on to the concrete slab to lap under the floor sheet membrane, **17**.

An additional precaution is to turn the floor dpm up the wall to top of screed level.

If the floor membrane is a sheet material and is at the same level as the wall dpc, the wall dpc may be specified wide enough to have about 75 mm projecting. This projecting material could then be stuck to the concrete and the floor membrane lapped and stuck on top. For this method to be successful, the dpc material must be thin and flexible, **18**.

If the floor dpm is a fluid type it will simply be continued up the wall to pass beyond the wall dpc, **19**.

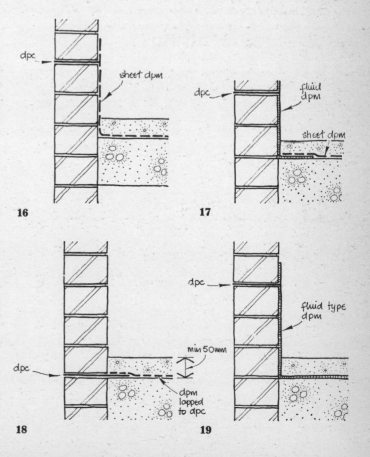

dpc — sheet dpm

dpc — fluid dpm

sheet dpm

16 **17**

dpc — fluid type dpm

dpc —

min 50mm

dpc — dpm lapped to dpc

18 **19**

Floor dpm as mastic immediately beneath floor finish

The Building Regulations permit 12·5 mm asphalt or pitchmastic as a dpm, for wood block flooring.

The mastic could be turned up the wall to pass beyond the wall dpc, but the thick mastic may result in a thickness problem with the skirting if wall is fair-faced or has a thin finish (see **21**).

Floor level above wall dpc

In all the above examples, it has been assumed that the inner wall dpc is above or at floor dpm level. With cavity wall construction this is normally so but with sloping sites and solid walls there may be situations where the wall dpc is *below* the floor dpm level. If this does occur, it is important to note that the vertical link must be formed *before* the oversite concrete is laid, **20**.

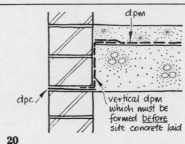

20

Vertical dpm problems

Damage Sheet material is liable to sitework damage which is unlikely to be made good unless supervision is strict.

Skirting fixing Wood skirtings often involve nailing through the vertical dpm. Penetration of dpm is usually accepted but damage may be less with fluid dpms than thin sheets.

Inside wall finish If the wall dpc is above skirting level, the vertical dpm may cause problems. With fair faced walling, this must be avoided.
With plastered walls, a sheet-type vertical dpm prevents adhesion of plaster. A bitumen solution type may be sanded immediately after application to assist adhesion. Alternatively, wire mesh can be used to provide a key.
A thick floor mastic continued up the wall as vertical dpm may force the skirting too far out from the wall, **21**.

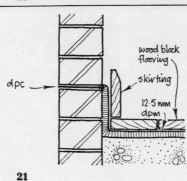

21

Cost considerations

The need for full protection against penetration of dampness is overriding. Consequential damage and repairs caused by dpc failure are many times more costly than if detailing and construction supervision had been correct in the first place. Cost is not usually a determining factor in the choice of dpc levels and details. It is only considered where the functional requirements can be met by a variety of materials, whose cost differentials, including labour, are shown in table I.

Table I Cost comparison of damp-proof courses*

Item	Index
Bitumen: hessian base	100
Bitumen: hessian base + lead	205
Pitch polymer	165
Two courses slates	615
There courseseng ineering brick	130 (allowing deduction for brickwork replaced)
Lead BS no 4	1160
Lead BS no 5	1400
Lead BS no 6	1620
Zinc 14 gauge	515
Aluminium 20 swg	585
Copper 24 swg	905
2000 gauge polythene	75

* Costs as at February 1974

Check list

Design
● Dpc levels related to *all* ground and paving levels
● Fix any change in level of dpc, considering appearance
● Internal dpc levels related to floor dpm and how continuity will be obtained
● Check all dpc levels with bottom of cavity level
● Check top of wall dpc joint to suit courses in wall for window openings and floors
● Consider external finish of dpc joint
● Determine type of dpc material considering: loading conditions, flexibility needs, possible wall movement, durability, effect on appearance, cost.

Specification
● Type and quality of material. (Note that Building Regulations allow liquid dpms of either 3 mm hot bitumen or coal tar pitch, or three coat solutions)
● Bedding, laps, forming steps, etc
● Method of joint to vertical or floor membrane
● Width related to wall width
● Draw, or cover by descriptions, all levels and details.

Supervision
● Check quality and width of materials
● Levels, related to ground, pavings, cavities and dpms
● Check cavity mortar droppings. The cavity must be inspected and cleaned out if necessary.
● Check joints and changes in levels
● Check exposed vertical dpcs for damage.

...

Timber framed walls: dpc at ground level

General considerations
Dpc design at the base of timber-framed walls must be carefully considered for the particular type of structure. Detailing will vary according to type of external cladding and type of floor construction, solid or suspended. Some constructions result in ground floors having to be raised considerably above ground level.
1 On sloping sites, positions where the dpc may be stepped are likely to be more restrictive than with masonry wall construction.
2 The *sequence* of building operations has important implications for detailing dpcs.

3 Illustrations **1** to **7** do *not* show wall structure, thermal insulation or vapour barriers.* Some form of insulation is almost always required. Internal vapour barriers are often necessary especially if the external wall covering is of a type through which water vapour cannot readily escape.
4 All vulnerable timbers such as wall plates, sill plates and sole plates should be pressure treated with a preservative even though they are partly protected by a dpc. Treatment of other timbers such as floor joists or wall framing may be worthwhile, depending on particular circumstances.

* MPBW Advisory Leaflet 79 *Vapour barriers*, HMSO

Timber frame/cavity/brick outer wall

Solid floor
Normal sequence of operations would be:
1 Lay foundation and oversite concrete.
2 Lay dpc beneath timber wall.
3 Erect timber wall.
4 Lay dpc beneath brick wall.
5 Build brick wall.
6 Lay floor dpm, followed by screed.

In **1**, if timber frames come prefabricated with breather paper *fixed*, the brick wall dpc cannot be correctly turned up behind it.
The horizontal brick wall dpc at bottom of cavity is a possible weakness. (See alternative in **2**.)
Mortar droppings must be completely and carefully removed from the bottom of the cavity.
Waterproofing of the site concrete by a dpm placed below the concrete would complicate the detail and seems unsuitable.
Care is needed to ensure proper continuity of external wall dpc and its upstand at corners.

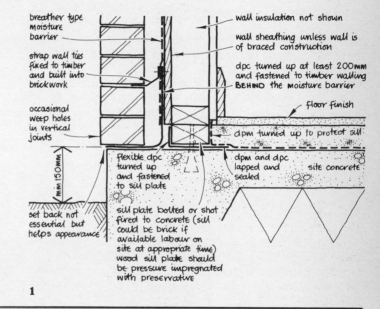

1

Solid floor and stepped concrete
Cavity and dpc relationship in **2** is better than method **1**.

Waterproofing of the site concrete by dpm placed below the concrete would again complicate the detail and seems unsuitable.

It may be difficult to place the fixing bolt near the edge of the concrete. One alternative may be some form of cranked strap.

On sloping sites, stepping would need careful consideration.

In **2**, breather paper *can* be fixed before arrival on site.

Kenneth Stevens, a student at Brighton Polytechnic, offered a solution in which a steel strap is cast into the concrete (next page).

Cecil Handisyde commented: 'If correctly positioned this would be satisfactory, but setting the strap in the concrete

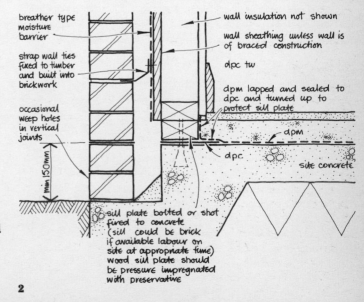

2

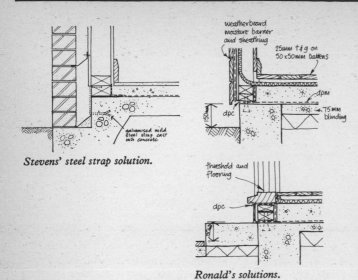

Stevens' steel strap solution.

Ronald's solutions.

to the exact level would need very good supervision, unless the material were thin enough to be bent to shape easily on site'.

R. E. Owen, senior lecturer in construction at Oxford Polytechnic, pointed out that the problem is dealt with on pages 18 and 19 of *Timber stud walls of Swedish redwood and whitewood* issued free by The Swedish Timber Council, Sweden House, 14 Trinity Square, London EC3N 4BN. He continued: 'In every case shown except one the fixing penetrates the horizontal dpc. In this exception a flat vertical strap is fixed, one assumes with a heavy screw or coach screw, to the back of the sole plate, where it would appear to interfere with the fixing of the inner wall lining. Moreover the strap is shown cast into the concrete slab, posing problems of vertical alignment, accuracy and location. My preferred solution would be a flat galvanised steel strap, about $250 \times 30 \times 3$ mm twice screwed to the underside of the plate and twice screwed to waterproof plugs in the concrete (or by the use of a pair of expanding bolts of appropriate size). This would give adequate location and restraint, unless the stud wall is subject to substantial lifting force. The tendency of the strap beneath the sole plate to overload the dpc material could be prevented by housing it in flush, or by using a thin strap packing between plate and dpc. However, the projection of the strap would have to be covered by screed and dpm. This detail would be unsuitable for power-floated concrete or an asphalt "screed" of only 12-15 mm. In my direct experience of fixing the plate by the

conventional rag-bolt through dpc and plate, it is quite easy and accurate either to place the bolts into the concrete slab while it is stiffening, or to cut mortices and grout in while the concrete is stiff but still soft. Locating the bolts 75 mm from the outer face is satisfactory and adequate for fixing into the 100 mm wide plate. A bituminous dpc gently pressed over each bolt tends to reseal around the bolt shank; pitch polymer or polythene probably would not.
'The bolt holes in the sole plate may be pre-drilled oversize to facilitate placing the plate on wall, and the nut tightened down over a large washer onto the sides of the hole.
'The full text of the Swedish booklet should be consulted for details.'

Richard Ronald, an architect in practice in London, sent sketches for a lightweight timber-frame structure with high insulation. There is a continuous dpm between blinding and floor slab. The slab is stepped back from the edge of the foundation: this allows the door threshold to be flush with the flooring, and continuous insulation between wall cavity and battened floor.

Cecil Handisyde commented: 'The published details did not include an example showing a timber floor on battens. The suggested detail exposes the full thickness of oversite concrete above the dpm. Unless the concrete is very well dried out before the flooring is laid moisture would be trapped in a stagnant air space. The outer cladding is brought to 150 mm above ground level. With vulnerable cladding the 200 mm dimension is preferable, but it was noted that one result of that dimension was to raise the level of the oversite concrete and therefore to increase the thickness and cost of hardcore. The detail proposed by Mr Ronald has a similar effect. As drawn the step detail could allow water penetration; a vertical dpc in front of the timber plates could usefully be included.'

The GLC commented: 'The details are sound. Bolting would be better than cranking for fixing plates to timber. Do not like the detail where the drainage fillet runs along the first brick jointing at ground level. Ground levels are rarely straight, even allowing for settlement of ground. The drainage fillet should always drain out any moisture at least one course above ground level, preferably two courses.'

Cecil Handisyde replied: 'Certainly care is needed to ensure that the levels shown are maintained. **2** makes this point with its 150 mm *minimum* for dpc level above ground. To implement the GLC suggestion would necessitate raising the level of the site slab relative to the ground, which would increase the cost.'

Suspended timber floor

Even with minimum underfloor space the finished floor level is raised appreciably above ground level which may be inconvenient.
In **3**, the cavity is sealed from the airbrick by a slate box with sides to prevent damp cavity air from entering joist space. Alternatively, the cavity could be sealed horizontally by placing adjoining bricks end-on, and vertically by bedding slates in the cavity across the bricks.
The air brick is dangerously close to ground level. It could be raised to above dpc if the timber plate of filling piece were cut.
In Scotland, solum and oversite concrete should be treated according to Building Standards (Scotland) Regulation G6.

The GLC commented: 'Slate is detailed but probably is rarely used these days. Polythene dpcs in the 2000 gauge range are suitable, having a roughened or textured surface.'

Cecil Handisyde replied: 'The text refers to slate only for forming the airbrick "duct".'

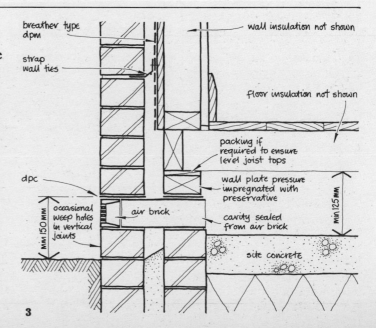

Timber frame/battens/tile hanging
Solid floor

In **4**, if timber wall frames come prefabricated and with moisture barrier already fixed, the bottom of wall flashing cannot be correctly positioned (unless the bottom 150 mm are left loose, and therefore vulnerable to damage).

Waterproofing of site concrete by a dpm placed below the concrete would complicate the detail and is not advised.

The projection of tiling beyond concrete base is useful in shadowing the edge of the concrete. Compare with **1**.

Tile hanging down to near ground level is subject to impact damage and would be unsuitable for some situations.
As in **2**, it may be difficult to place the fixing bolt near the edge of the concrete.

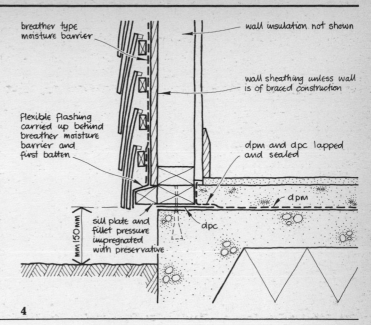

4

Suspended timber floor

Breather type moisture barrier is carried down in front of the flexible flashing in **5**. This makes on-site fixing of the moisture barrier essential.

Tile hanging down near ground level is subject to impact damage and would be unsuitable for some conditions.

The airbrick in **5** is dangerously close to ground level and may become blocked.

This can only be improved by raising the whole structure by an extra brick course.

In Scotland, solum and oversite concrete should be treated according to Building Standards (Scotland) Regulation G6.

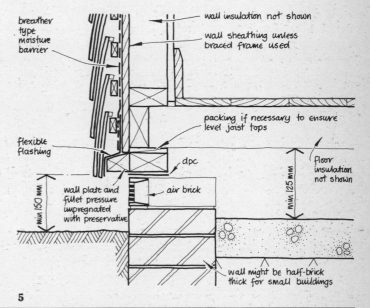

5

Timber frame/timber cladding
Solid floor

In **6**, it is assumed that timber cladding provides bracing, so timber sheathing shown next to framing on **1** to **5** is omitted. If cladding is inadequate, bracing by sheathing or in the frame construction must be included. Battens are not shown. They would be needed for vertical board cladding and have the advantages of forming an additional cavity which would improve insulation.

If cladding is of an almost impervious type, condensation on its inner face may occur unless there is either a ventilated air space behind the cladding or an effective moisture barrier on the inside of the walling.

To reduce risk of damage by splashing, timber cladding is kept 200 mm above ground level. The top of site concrete, and floor level, are therefore higher than in other examples. This probably means extra hardcore thickness at increased cost.

As with earlier examples the placing of site dpm below the concrete would cause problems.
As in **2** and **4**, it may be difficult to place the fixing bolt near the edge of the concrete.

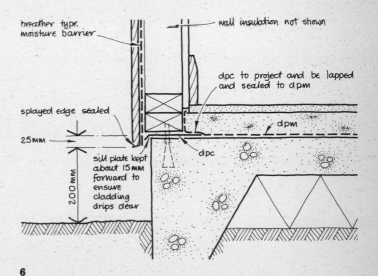

6

Raising the cladding to 200 mm minimum above ground level reduces the risk of damage, but the exposed bottom edge of the cladding is still vulnerable and must be protected (ie cut ends of treated timber should be retreated).

Suspended timber floor

In **7**, it is assumed that timber cladding provides bracing so timber sheathing shown next to framing on **1** to **5** is omitted. If cladding is inadequate bracing by sheathing or in the frame construction must be included.

Battens are not shown. They would be needed for vertical board cladding and have the advantage of forming an additional cavity which would improve insulation.

In this detail floor level inevitably becomes high above ground level.

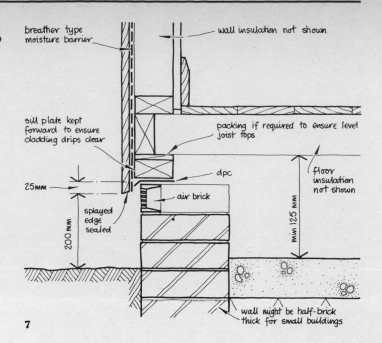

breather type moisture barrier

wall insulation not shown

sill plate kept forward to ensure cladding drips clear

packing if required to ensure level joist tops

25mm

dpc

floor insulation not shown

air brick

min 125 mm

splayed edge sealed

200 mm

wall might be half-brick thick for small buildings

7

7

Masonry walls: jambs with timber window frames

Old and new construction

In traditional construction most window and many door frames were fixed into a reveal formed in the stone or brick of a solid wall, **1**. The reason for this may have been partly aesthetic, a desire to hide the considerable width of a boxed sash window, but the effect was to protect the wall/frame joint from the worst of direct driving rain. On the other hand, the solid masonry provided no dpm between the exterior wet wall and the timber. In many areas windows are now built in as masonry rises, but the old system of fixing later prevails in some regions, eg Scotland.
In traditional construction softwood was often of high quality, wood sills were frequently of durable oak and quite often a stone sub-sill was used.

Modern construction is very different, and experience has shown that water penetration often causes untreated woodwork to rot; also if water reaches the interior of walls, it damages structure or decoration, **2**.

Although this detail deals specifically with jambs, the designer must also consider their relation to head and sill details. For example, sill and head detailing will be affected if the frame is positioned to suit a masonry jamb reveal or placed wholly behind the line of a vertical dpm in a cavity

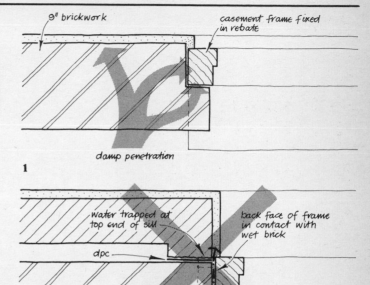

9" brickwork
casement frame fixed in rebate
damp penetration
1

water trapped at top end of sill
back face of frame in contact with wet brick
dpc
passage of water between window frame and wall
2

wall (see detail 11, page 52, 'Window sills', and detail 12, page 58, 'External doorways', for effect on door opening of door frame position).

The jamb

For the jamb detail alone the following points should be considered:

Degree of site exposure

Types of proposed materials
Water penetration through masonry can vary considerably. A dense 'impermeable' brick may leak through joint shrinkage and fail to dry out, whereas an apparently permeable material may prove less troublesome because, although it gets very wet, it also dries quickly.

Timber could be durable hardwood or preservative treated softwood, but not unprotected softwood of poor quality.

All lugs and fixings must be galvanised.

Mastic must be backed with plastic foam except on very small windows where mastic is forming a seal only and is not likely to be stressed by movement of frame **3**.

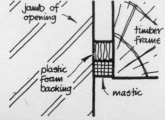

jamb of opening
timber frame
plastic foam backing
mastic
3

Workmanship
Some details depend for success upon careful workmanship. The building type may decide what quality of labour and supervision can be expected, and details should be chosen accordingly.

Order of fixing
Details suited to frames 'built-in' as the masonry goes up do not always work for frames which are to be 'fixed' after the masonry opening is complete.

Position of frame in wall
Whether in a reveal.
Where in relation to wall vertical dpm.

Prevention of water reaching to inside of structure

Protection of back of frame from dampness
either entering directly into frame/wall joint
or penetrating front face masonry and reaching the frame.

Appearance and convenience
Appearance is affected by width of visible frame and distance of frame from wall faces.

Convenient position of windows, size of inside window board and fixing curtains relative to opening lights, possible angle of door opening are all affected by position of frame in wall.

Position of dpc
Whatever detail of window opening, dpc must be brought
through to end of wall as otherwise water can pass to inner
skin causing deterioration of plaster, **4**.

This is a common fault on sites although dpc has been
detailed to come up to face of brickwork.

Where joints in vertical dpc occur, the dpc material on the
upper piece must lap to the external face of lower piece
of dpc, **5**.

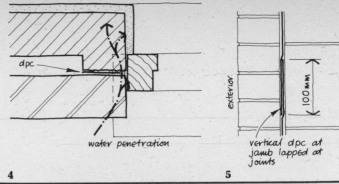

4

5

Wall to frame joint
Straight joint: no fill

In **6** brickwork is built up tight to frame as work proceeds.
Dpc is brought up tight to back of frame (continual care is
required).

Softwood sill is stopped at face of brick opening and joint
filled with mastic. Sill should only be built in if made of
oak or other water-resistant hardwood (shown dotted).

Softwood frame must be pressure treated against rot with a
preservative which can be painted. Back face of frame and
end of sill should be given full paint treatment.

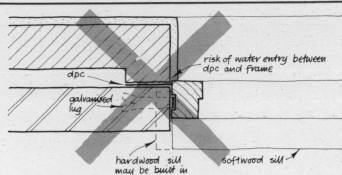

6

6 should only be employed on very sheltered sites. It *must
not* be used with hard service engineering, or similar hard,
non-porous bricks, or recessed joints.

Straight joint: dpc wraps round
brickwork

A more positive water barrier may be obtained by use of a
flexible dpc such as 2000 gauge polythene extended along
back face of frame, **7**, but barrier will be broken where
fixings occur. If however dpc is first fixed to frame, lugs
may be screw-fixed to frame through dpc and the resulting
puncture will not matter. (It may be difficult to avoid
damage to a flexible dpc pre-fixed to the frame.)
Frame must be kept away from face of brickwork to allow
proper mastic joint including foam plastic backing, **3**.

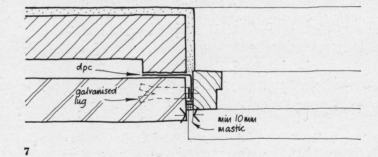

7

Dpc must be fixed tight to frame face as otherwise this may
be damaged when mastic backing piece is applied. A
flexible type of dpc is required.

7 and **8** cannot be used when frame is fixed after opening
is formed.

If windows are 'specials', a detail similar to **7** may be
altered to assist in building brickwork to frame, by rebating
corner to receive mastic, **8**.

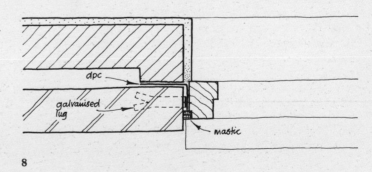

8

Straight joint:
dpc projects into frame

It would seem possible to achieve positive seal by
projecting a fairly stiff dpc into recess in back of frame, **9**.
But it is difficult to fix the frame in this position. The dpc
material must be wider than the normal half brick wall type
if it is to give full protection to walling and project into
frame.

Window can be moved further back, and if front of frame is
rebated, dpc can project into recess, and the face can be

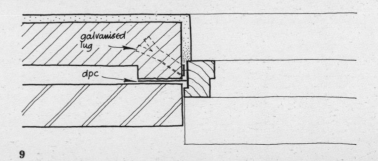

9

sealed with mastic backed with foam strip, **10a**, or cover strip, **10b**, (costing 25 per cent less than **10a**).

Frame can be fixed with lug as brickwork proceeds, or be inserted later and screw-fixed.

Good fixing to dry brickwork can be achieved.

The whole of the back face of frame is dry and not in contact with wet brickwork.

A wide external sill will result (see detail 11, page 52).

The previous detail, **10**, can be modified for fixing frame into prepared opening but junction with dpc is not so positive, **11**. (Could be adapted as **8** to allow mastic to project into groove in frame.)

Dpc should be left projecting from wall only a small amount, as otherwise it is likely to be damaged before or during window fixing.

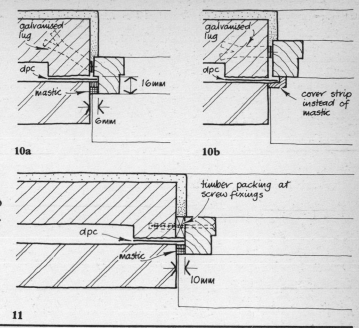

10a   **10b**

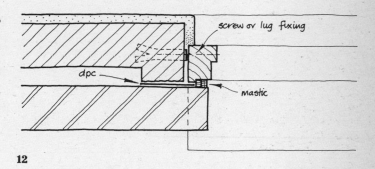

11

Frame set in wall rebate

Forming a wall rebate, **12**, gives the best weatherproof joint, but the inner leaf opening must be dimensioned for frame space requirement. If that was modular then external wall opening would not be.

If using mastic, the difficulty is to make a satisfactory joint between bpc and mastic pointing.

If dpc is brought through to face of brickwork opening no satisfactory joint can be obtained.

If frame is rebated on front face or piece of ply fixed to face, frame can be pressed against dpc and positive gap formed for filling with mastic.

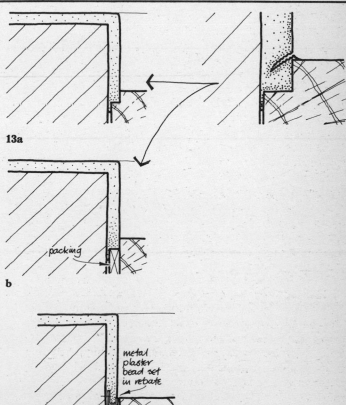

12

Plaster finish to frame

Whether details **13a** or **b** are used, plaster will not be finished true to frame and will crack when frame shrinks.

The simple butt joint to frame is no worse.

Only a cover strip will prevent one seeing the inevitable crack, **13c**.

With good workmanship, a plaster bead provides a satisfactory finish in the form of a controlled crack, **13d**. It can also be used with a rebated frame, **13e**.

Plymouth architect, **Michael Boulesteix**, objected to stopping the vertical dpc flush with the brickwork and insisted that it should be taken into the cavity: 'It is standard practice in this office to project vertical

13a

b

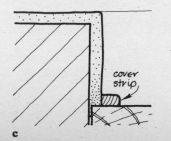

c

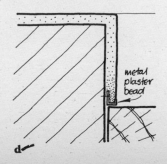

d

e

damp-proof courses at least 4in into the cavity beyond the closing walls, as shown on the attached sketches (right).
'We have learned from bitter experience that the usual method of stopping the dpc at the same width as the closing inner leaf is totally inadequate in the conditions of severe exposure we have to design for in the West Country. Wind-driven rain can by-pass the dpc across a perfect bridge.
'We know because we have had to pay for rectifying damage caused in this way in adopting the typical and usual detail repeated in your sketches.
'We specify a "Hyload"* or LD.20E dpc which is suitable for these purposes, and check very carefully during site supervision that the details are carried out as drawings, as the bricklayers do not usually understand the reason until it is explained to them.'

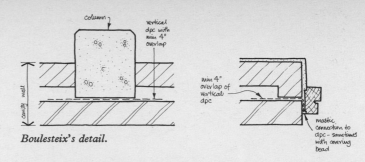

Boulesteix's detail.

Cecil Handisyde commented: 'This is a good point and one made also in the next letter by London architect, Tom Kay of Tom Kay Associates, although I question the practicability of Kay's second point.

Tom Kay wrote: 'Vertical dpcs have a habit of slipping sideways whilst being built into window jambs of cavity walls causing bridging of the cavity. For this reason I have always specified dpcs to be 2in wider than the cavity closer (plus any return behind the frame, required by the design). I also think that you were wrong to show the dpc stopping short of the pointing mastic in **7** and **8**, since water can get to the back of the frame and be trapped behind the foam and mastic pointing.'

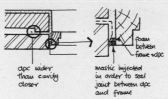

Kay's jamb details.

Another West Country architect, **Sam Webb** of Taunton thinks that only **12** is to be recommended. He wrote:
'One of the failures of much modern building is due to the details used in your examples **7, 8, 9, 10a, 10b** and **11**.
'Whereas water may be stopped entering at the jamb it will still nevertheless run down the edges of the sill and rot the timber. A window of course has three separate details, head, sill and jamb, and in just showing the jamb detail it could set a dangerous precedent in that the other two conditions are not considered. **12** is about the only waterproof detail shown. It gives:

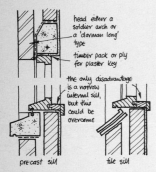

Webb's head and sill details.

1 a positive lapped seal not a butt joint;
2 the mastic is protected against the weather;
3 it could be pointed with cement mortar;
4 all other details are vulnerable to water penetration if the joint shrinks. If this frame shrinks there is ample protection.
5 the dpc is straight, there is little danger of damage and it is not penetrated by fixings;
6 the edge of the sill is protected;
7 there is a sliding tolerance which provides ample play for taking up tolerances in manufacture;
8 the outside brick wall can be dimensioned to brick sizes. This should be the modular size. The disadvantage of the detail as drawn is the deep wooden sill.
'This is easily overcome by using either an undersill of two courses of tiles or a precast concrete sill (left). This will avoid warping or cracking of a wide sill. Of course both these examples are more expensive than a plain wide timber sill but I feel that the subsequent savings in repairs will more than offset this extra in the life of the building.'

Cecil Handisyde commented: 'The need to consider head and sill in relation to jamb is referred to but, for convenience, the treatments are dealt with separately in details 10 and 11 (pages 47 and 52).'

Hugo Mason commented: 'I am surprised by some of the window reveal details you have shown. Although you make reference to workmanship and site exposure, I must say from my own experience I find many of your details unsatisfactory.
'We must consider that a building is to be permanent and the mastic shown on your details invariably fails after a few years. This would almost certainly lead to a failure in **7, 8, 10a** and **11**. A joint must be considered waterproof before the application of mastic.
'**9** does not take account of poor workmanship or a flexible dpc. Invariably there will be gaps between the dpc and the frame because a dpc is rarely truly vertical.
'**10b** can also be considered as temporary. On exposed sites slender cover fillets do not stand up to water penetration and a crack between the frame and the fillet in this instance would certainly allow water penetration.

'I am sorry to be so critical, but I have seen most of these details fail in practice. I enclose a sketch (below) of a window reveal detail which we find satisfactory in all conditions.'

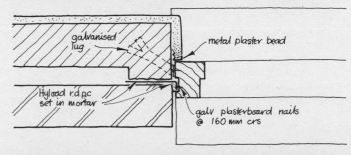

* Agrément Certificate 75/291 for the Hyload dpc system replaces 73/173 and relates to its use in both solid and cavity construction in horizontal, vertical or stepped positions, including cavity trays. The certificate now covers the complete system including Hyload pre-formed cloaks for corner details and changes of level, and Hyload Contact Adhesive for sealing all lap joints.

8

Masonry walls: metal windows fixed direct

Fixing

Jamb, head and sill details depend upon whether windows are fixed as brickwork is being built, or fixed subsequently to prepared window openings. In the latter, accurate masonry dimensions must be obtained and very careful site supervision is needed to ensure this.

In domestic work frames are often fixed by the general contractor as the work proceeds. On larger buildings, windows are usually fixed in prepared openings, sometimes by the general contractor but often by a window specialist.

BS 990 (Part 1 1967, Part 2 1972)* gives standard sizes and fixing positions for domestic windows. Where non-standard windows are to be built into prepared openings, it is essential that full window details (architects' or manufacturers' drawings) are issued to the contractor so that openings can be accurately formed, and, when appropriate, fixing blocks can be cast into the structure.

Where special windows are to be fixed it is usually preferable for the manufacturer to fix as, if any defect appears later, there is no risk of a demarcation dispute between manufacturer and contractor.

The main considerations are:
1 strength of fixing
2 efficient weatherproofing around the frame perimeter.
Details which may have proved successful in low buildings on relatively sheltered sites may be inadequate in a higher building, or on severely exposed or seaside areas. (See Elder, A. J., and Vandenberg, M., *AJ Handbook of Building Enclosure*, page 168ff, IS 'External Walls 9'. The Architectural Press Ltd. 1974.)

Because of the difficulty in making a satisfactory metal frame to masonry joint, steel windows are often fixed in timber sub-frames. Fixing of sub-frame then follows wood windows detailing (detail 7, page 29).

Jamb details

Window manufacturers often provide very good details of the way in which windows can be fixed to the structure but they do not always indicate the relationship of the frame to dpm systems.

1 is a typical example. The fixing is adequate, but if the internal plaster were in contact with external brickwork disaster would result.

The architect must carefully appraise any details he takes from a catalogue to ensure the details apply satisfactorily to his situation.

Inside
plaster
waterproof cement
mastic
WATER
Outside

1

* British Standards Institution, 2 Park Street, London W.1

Fixing methods
When frame is built in, it is difficult to maintain a constant 3 mm (the old $\frac{3}{32}$in) gap. Invariably brickwork is built tight to frame. Mastic then becomes only an applied fillet.

Even with a 3 mm gap the mastic joint is of doubtful efficiency. Better protection can be obtained if the vertical dpc is extended into the frame, as in **2**.

This limits the position of the frame in the thickness of the wall.

Built-in lug fixing
In **2** the lug is bolted to the frame and built in as work proceeds. Security of fixing depends upon careful workmanship when bedding the lugs, as they are at the edge of a brick joint. A cranked lug would overcome this difficulty. Not suitable when interior walling is fair faced (see **3**). Lugs should preferably be at centres which are a multiple of the brick course dimension.

Built-in lug fixing for fair-faced inside wall
A rebate is needed, **3**. Where space between windows is big enough, the differing plan dimensions of inner and outer leaves of a cavity wall may be obtained by easing vertical joint widths. Where piers between windows are small, the outer leaf dimension should suit brick size and the inner leaf may need cut bricks or blocks.

Screw fixing
Frames can be screw-fixed direct to structure. It is not possible to do this with cavity wall construction as the screw fixing would coincide or be very close to the vertical dpc. In fixing to concrete, the frame can be screw-fixed using cast-in plugs or drilled holes and plugs. If face of concrete is rebated as **4a** and frame is fully bedded in mastic, a good waterproof barrier between frame and structure is provided. This also applies to **4b** where frame is fixed to timber.

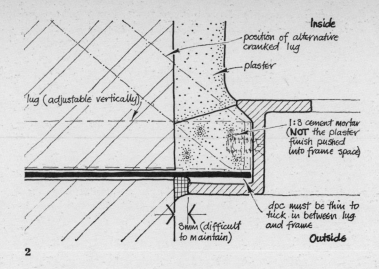

2

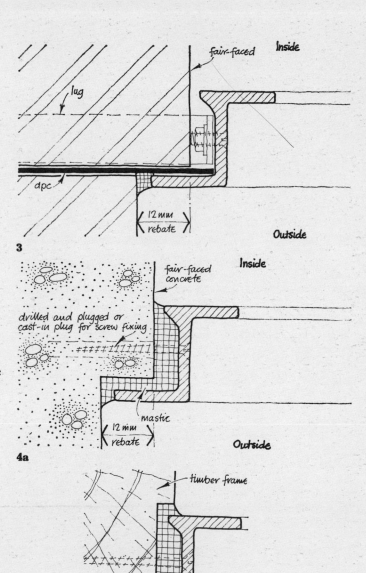

3

4a

4b

4c appears in BS 990. To be successful, the cement filling
and pointing must be carried out perfectly. There is a
risk of differential movement between window and
structure which may cause breakage of cement and mastic
joints. This detail depends on narrow mastic pointing
rather than a 'designed' mastic joint and could break down
very quickly. The detail becomes worse if the face is only as
much as 5 or 6 mm out of position. Protection then depends
on wider mastic joint, which may, unless carefully
supervised, be little more than a mastic coating on the
cement backing.

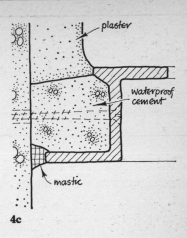

4c

Lug fixing screwed to structure

Lugs bolted to the metal frame are used to obtain a fixing
away from the line of window, and are covered by the
internal wall finish, **5**. The lug is screwed to the structure or
shot-fixed. The cavity wall dpc may be brought into the
frame but is liable to damage when the frame is placed in
position, particularly as the lugs will already be fixed to
frame. A thin, flexible dpc such as polythene is preferable.
Screws should be non-rusting. (**5b** shows rebated cavity
wall.)

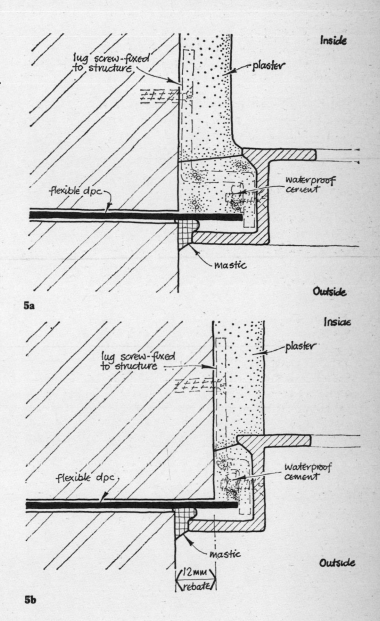

5a

5b

Sill details

Brick sill

Lugs may be built into brick or tile sills, **6**. It is difficult to hold the dpc in position while frame is bedded and to fill the bottom section with mortar. Dpcs across bottom of window opening must lap behind vertical dpcs at jambs.

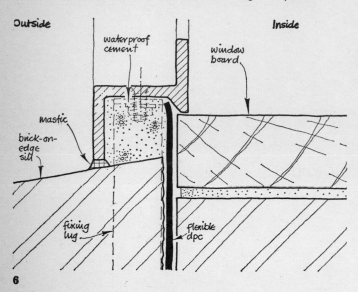

Outside — *Inside*

water proof cement · window board · mastic · brick-on-edge sill · fixing lug · flexible dpc

6

Concrete sill

In cavity wall construction, the position of frame relative to sill is controlled by the jamb detail. The cavity must be continuous immediately under the sill, **8**.

Metal sill

Pressed metal sills may be used, bolted to the frame using lug fixing bolts, **7**. As the upstanding dpc may be damaged while the window is fixed, a flexible type such as polythene is preferable.

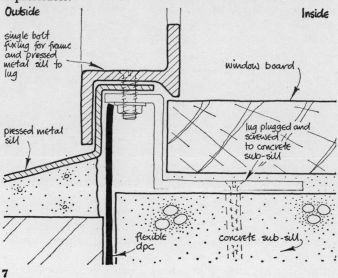

Outside — *Inside*

single bolt fixing for frame and pressed metal sill to lug · window board · pressed metal sill · lug plugged and screwed to concrete sub-sill · flexible dpc · concrete sub-sill

7

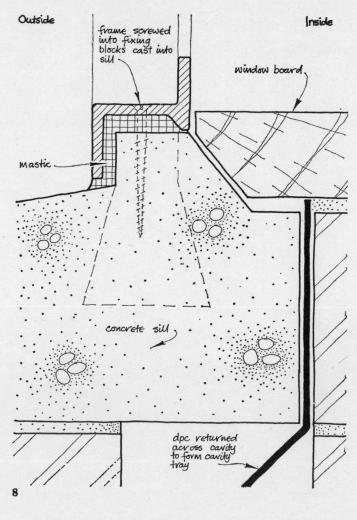

Outside — *Inside*

frame screwed into fixing blocks cast into sill · window board · mastic · concrete sill · dpc returned across cavity to form cavity tray

8

These details were criticised by **P. Ashworth,** of Stocksfield, Northumberland, for being 'vulnerable to water and damp penetration'. He made the following points:

'1 If jamb detail, **1,** is described as unsatisfactory from a water penetration point of view, surely the same comment should apply to details **4a, 4c** and **9** because the concrete has not been described as being waterproof.

2 In concrete sill detail, **8,** the dpc is shown protecting the inner leaf of brickwork from contact with the 'wet' concrete sill, but no attempt is made to protect the more vulnerable timber window board from the same source of dampness.

3 In metal sill detail, **7,** the problem of the upstanding dpc is referred to. Surely in view of the position of the pressed metal sill the dpc only needs to come up to the top of the concrete sub-sill anyway?

4 None of the details take account of the effect of cold bridging, inner leafs are shown as concrete or brick, never insulating blocks, and the details showing plastered reveals to concrete surrounds should surely be amended to show an insulated lining to avoid condensation.'

Philip Berry and **Cecil Handisyde** commented:

'1 True, the concrete is not described as waterproof, but good quality concrete has sufficient resistance to water to prevent penetration to plaster.

2 Fair comment—the dpc could be brought on to the top face of the sill to protect the timber.

3 The vertical dpc should project above the bottom edge of the window, particularly if there are joints in the length of the sill.

4 This sheet aimed to show the relationship between dpc, frame and wall, etc. Insulating materials for linings and inner leafs may be desirable, but would not affect these relationships.'

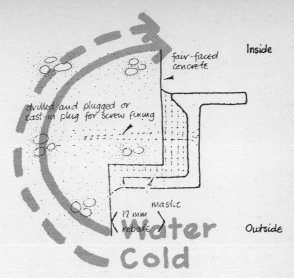

Original **4a** *with Ashworth's amendment.*

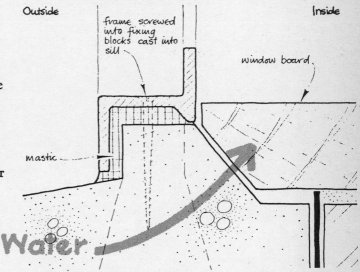

Original **8** *with Ashworth's amendment.*

Window heads

Concrete lintels
The lintel must be positively throated to ensure that water does not run back to the vulnerable joint between window and structure, **9**.

No fixings should be made to prestressed lintels without first reaching agreement with the lintel manufacturer.

Metal lintels
With steel or pressed metal lintels, **10, 11,** it is not usually possible to screw through the window frame direct to structure; plugs or fixing blocks are required to allow screw fixing at a suitable position.

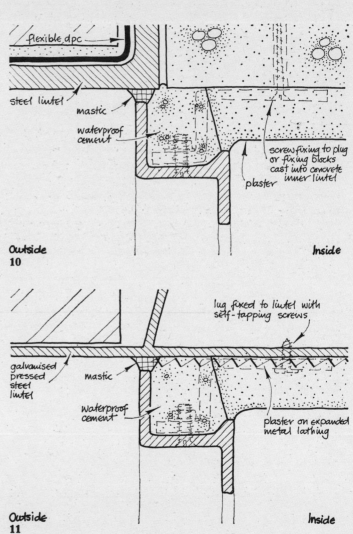

9 throat — mastic — frame screwed into plug or fixing blocks cast into concrete head — plaster — waterproof cement — Outside — Inside

10 flexible dpc — steel lintel — mastic — waterproof cement — plaster — screw fixing to plug or fixing blocks cast into concrete inner lintel — Outside — Inside

11 galvanised pressed steel lintel — mastic — waterproof cement — lug fixed to lintel with self-tapping screws — plaster on expanded metal lathing — Outside — Inside

9

Tile hanging and timber cladding

Construction

Traditional details which at one time appeared to give acceptable results may not satisfy modern conditions. As a result construction changes may have been introduced without all implications being fully appreciated. For example 9in solid walling was commonly used for small buildings, but as rooms were ventilated by chimneys and ill-fitting windows this not entirely damp-proof construction was fairly acceptable. Now a cavity wall construction is regarded as essential for most exposed masonry walls. Returning to solid wall construction, with cladding on the outside, may seem to offer reasonable economy but now the solid wall might be both thinner and of a different material from the traditional type. The result may be entirely satisfactory for general walling areas but the change may make traditional detailing around openings unsuitable. Careful judgment of conditions of site exposure is required when considering the details shown below.

Tile hanging on masonry walls

In old work vertical tiling was sometimes nailed direct to brick joints. Rat-trap brick bond was sometimes used to form joints at a convenient 4½in (114 mm) vertical spacing. Direct nailing of tiles to some types of lightweight concrete walling is possible, but the usual method is to nail to wood battens and only this system is dealt with here.

Battens are usually 40 mm × 20 mm and should always be pressure impregnated with preservative. Horizontal battens are generally fixed either to brick or block vertical joints or by direct nailing to blocks, when these are of suitable material to hold nails. Vertical counterbattens increase cost and are now seldom used. Check that there is no reaction between the preservative and aluminium alloy nails.

Window and door openings

The position of the frame in relation to the wall face considerably affects appearance, cost and detailing necessary to ensure a weatherproof result.

In **1a** the frame projects and tiles butt against it. Unless the frame is of deep section, it is difficult to fix.

In **1b**, the frame is set back. Tiles return into the jamb. This detail is occasionally seen with thick walling in old buildings; it is scarcely ever used now because there is insufficient return wall to make it worth while, and a thick frame is needed to receive tiling.

Frame is flush with wall face in **1c**. Frame fixing is no problem but weatherproofing is less satisfactory than in **1d** (see **7** and **8** for enlarged details).

In **1d** the frame projects to line with front of tiling battens. Weatherproofing is easier than in **1c** but the frame may need to be thicker (see also **9**).

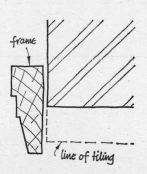

1a

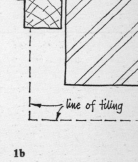

1b

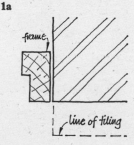

1c

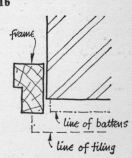

1d

Tile cladding with frames projecting

Details as **2a** and **2b** have been used but:

1 A very deep frame is necessary.

2 It is feasible to form the flashing into such a shape only if lead is used.

3 It is important to achieve an absolutely tight lead-to-frame joint. A near-tight joint lets water in but prevents it drying out again.

4 Vertical stop battens should be positioned to suit holes in tiles, otherwise fixing with one nail only results in end tiles drooping.

5 If frame head and side members are of similar section the tiling over the head projects beyond the normal tiling line and an awkward junction occurs, **3**. (A skilful tiler can effect the change by sweeping the tiles from one plane to the other.)

Preferred alternative to **2a** (jamb) is **4**. This overcomes most of the drawbacks of method **2** and the flashing can be made with any sheet dpc material, but a standard-depth frame may still not be adequate for easy and secure fixing. Ends of tiling should be pointed in a mix not stronger than 1:1:6. Pointing may require renewal at intervals but this will not be critical or difficult. The wall side of the frame cannot be repainted.

If the plan of the jamb used is as shown in **2a** an alternative head detail is as shown in **5**. This keeps tiling over the head in the same plane as general wall tiling, but a lead flashing would be expensive and any alternative would possibly not look very attractive. In **5** the head of the frame can either project beyond the jambs or be stopped on the same line.

R. E. Owen wrote: 'Figures **2a** and **4** are not satisfactory. Both show a deep and wasteful wood window frame section. In **2a** a sealed lead to back of frame junction is not possible, even if the vertical lead dpc is closely nailed to frame. The vertical dpc must be fixed before the window frame is built in, so that it projects unsupported and is vulnerable to damage until battening and tiling are done. In the attached sketch (*shown right*) a normal profile window frame is used with a prepainted tongued-in lining fixed later. The no 3 lead secret gutter is folded into the groove. The back of the lining is protected and a margin is accessible for repainting. A single copper clout nail to the top of the vertical batten, holds the leadwork. Note that the nibs projecting from the backs of the tiles may foul the vertical batten.'

Cecil Handisyde replied: 'Mr Owen's alternative to **2a** seems a good idea, but how is the added member fixed?— it appears to be shown free to move.'

Sill detail

It is questionable whether lead apron flashing is always really necessary, as a wood sill, **6ab**, projecting beyond the line of tiling and incorporating a good throat, provides fairly good shelter to the bed joint of sill to wall, provided that it has a reasonable slope and the paint film is maintained intact (but top tile facing nails will be exposed). Clearly protection by a flashing is more necessary if the wall is of solid construction and of porous material than if it is of cavity construction. If a flashing is used it is easier to fix if carried back and turned up behind the sill as in **6a**, rather than turned up into a groove in the sill, **6b**: **6ab** assume that window height coincides with tile coursing.

The method in **6ab** is commonly used but can look crude unless well done. The bottom edge of the lead is often

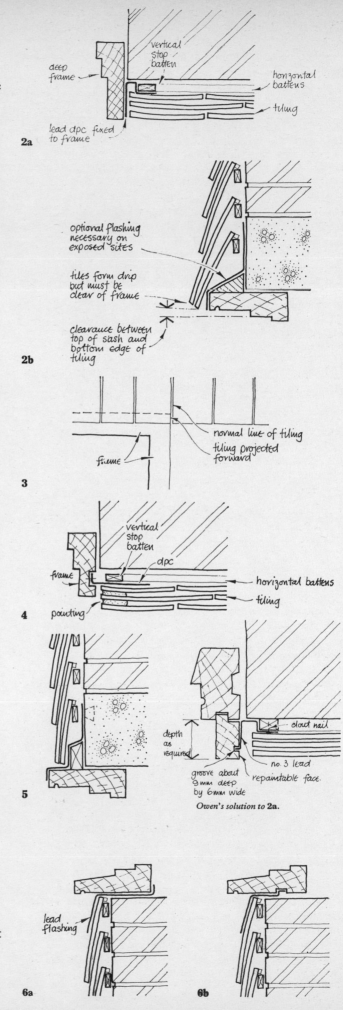

Owen's solution to **2a**.

scalloped to improve appearance. It is possible to hide a lead apron by drawing it down the wall face and then over the second tile. This is a good solution, but it involves fixing the lead first, then fixing the top batten between laying the second and top tile courses (a less expensive material than lead could be used).

R. E. Owen commented: 'In **6a** the reason for the deep lead flashing as shown is that it must cover the open vertical butt joints between tiles in the top course, as there is no layer of tiles with staggered joints behind them to prevent water penetration. To avoid using a deep lead flashing a strip of bituminous felt is clout nailed to the top batten before the tiles are hung, thus backing up the dry vertical joints. A small width of lead flashing fixed later masks the tiling nails.' (See Owen's solution right.)

Cecil Handisyde replied: 'The alternative to **6a** is a good one and is probably cheaper, as less lead is used.'

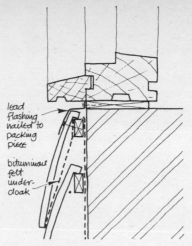

*Owen's solution to **6a**.*

Tile cladding with frame flush
With the frame flush or almost flush, with the main wall face a standard size frame can be easily fixed to the wall. With the frame flush with the wall face a detail as in **7** is possible but the exposed vertical batten is unsatisfactory.

An alternative to **7** is to stop horizontal battens just short of the end of the tiles and point up the gap, **8**.

If end tiles are to be properly nailed the battens cannot stop much more than 15 mm short of the tiles, so the space for pointing is small and the material may fall out. Success of this method depends on the mix used and on workmanship; instead filling with a non-hardening mastic should be considered.

In both **7** and **8** the joint between frame and wall is exposed and, if the walling is solid, risk of rain penetration at such joints is greater than in a cavity wall in which a detail with vertical dpc can be included.

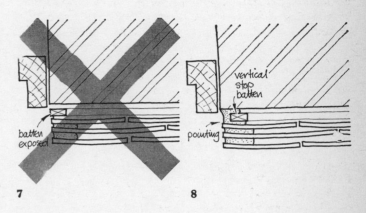

Frame slightly projecting
Method **9** may involve using a somewhat thicker frame with some increase in cost, but it overcomes the problems shown in **7** and **8**.

Head detail
With a flush frame there is no prop to hold out the bottom of the tiling so something must be provided. A detail such as **10a** has often been used.

The projecting tiles can be fixed in only after the frame is in position, therefore a good joint and fixing are difficult to obtain.

A projecting head of the type shown in **2b** and **5** could be used, or a fillet as in **10b**.

R. E. Owen said: 'Detail **10b** will be unsightly. The view from beneath reveals a vertical concrete lintel face and the underside of a sawn tilting fillet. The tilting fillet should be lowered to mask the concrete to frame joint and have its underside planed and painted or stained.'

Cecil Handisyde replied: 'It *would* improve the appearance of the tilting fillet in **10b** if the underside were planed and painted, but it need not necessarily be lowered, as the heavy shadow would obscure concrete frame joint anyway.'

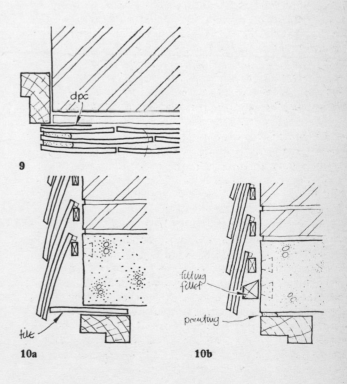

Sill detail
A projecting sill as in **6** is the best treatment even if the frame otherwise is flush or nearly flush with the wall. (Alternatively a sub-sill can be used.)

Eaves finish

A top flashing over the tiling is sometimes recommended. This seems unnecessary if tiles are carried above an eaves soffit, **11**.

The eaves soffit is unlikely to finish flush to the tiling. The space left may provide useful ventilation for the eaves but the gap should not be wide enough for birds or vermin to enter: ie not more than 12 mm.

With a flat roof the top of the tiling may not be protected unless some form of cover flashing is provided.

External angles

Mitred plain tiles with soakers and tiling finishing on a timber corner post are seldom used now. The usual method is to use special corner tiles which bond with ordinary tiling and present no difficulties.

Abutments

When tiling finishes against a projecting pier or a return wall a flashing, **12**, is usually the best method but a cheap job can be made by pointing only (resulting in higher maintenance costs).

Properly done, such a flashing would be in conjunction with soakers. Traditionally **12a** has been used at all intersections of tiling and masonry. It costs more but is time-tested and secure.

There may be a case for the treatment in **12** if the projecting masonry is considered to give adequate resistance to rain penetration, and when the tiled back-up wall is much less resistant (eg 150 mm of porous brick walling as in **13**).

Setting out

Although horizontal spacing of tiles can be slightly adjusted by *increasing* width of joints between tiles, this increase cannot reasonably amount to more than about 20 mm in a metre length. Tile cutting is expensive and often ugly and should be avoided by carefully calculating all horizontal dimensions to suit tile sizes, with some additional tolerances for openings.

Cost comparisons

Comparisons between tile hanging and other finishes depend upon various details in addition to the direct relation of cost of tiling to other basic wall finishes. For example:

A cheaper solid wall may be substituted for a cavity wall or, as in many old buildings, a frame structure may be used. Some dpcs may be eliminated eg over lintels and in jambs, but in some cases expensive dpcs may be required because of the tiling.

Frames may need to be thicker or deeper than usual and may be appreciably more expensive because they are non-standard, and use more material.

Horizontal dimensions to suit tiling may differ from requirements elsewhere: additional expense could be caused by the need for cutting bricks or blocks, or for varying sizes of frames.

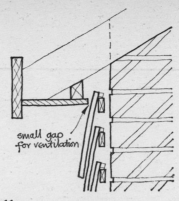

small gap for ventilation

11

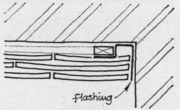

flashing

12

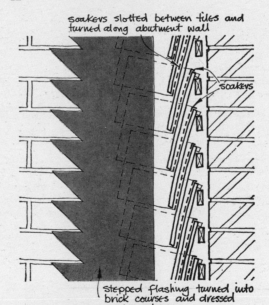

soakers slotted between tiles and turned along abutment wall

soakers

stepped flashing turned into brick courses and dressed over soakers

12a

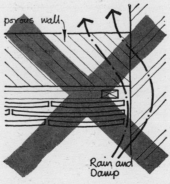

porous wall

Rain and Damp

13

Tile hanging on timber frame walls

If water penetrates to a timber frame it may be more serious than in a masonry wall, but because of the wood-to-wood joints some details become rather easier to form.

Projecting frame
The rebated frame is fixed to cover moisture barrier, **14**. If tiling above the opening is to line through with general wall tiling, the problem is similar to that in masonry walls and **5** might be used. Note however that the lead should be fixed *behind* the moisture barrier as in **15**.

A head detail, **16**, would be simple for a frame kept back to line with the sheathing but at jambs the batten ends would be exposed and a vertical batten would be necessary, **7**.

External corners of buildings will normally be made with corner tiles, as in masonry backing. Abutments to projecting masonry walls produce the usual timber frame/masonry wall joint problem but, if anything, the tiling helps to shield that joint and certainly does not add difficulties.

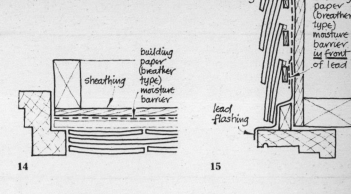

14

15

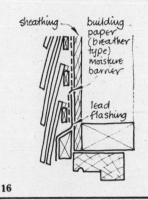

16

Timber cladding on masonry walls

There is a choice of joint shapes for board-to-board junctions, which may affect the rain-proof qualities of the cladding, but there are important differences between vertical and horizontal boarding. Vertical boarding provides a flat back and flat front surface, an end finish unbroken by joints and no exposed end grain. Horizontal boarding can provide flat front and back surfaces but as it has horizontal joints, it may have gaps and will then have exposed end grain, **17**.

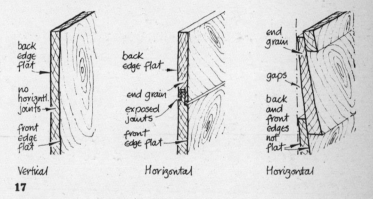

Vertical

Horizontal

Horizontal

17

Jambs
The frame must be wide enough to allow the end board to be nailed to it, **18**. This method is not suitable for horizontal boards because of end grain exposure.

The method shown in **19** gives rather better protection to the frame/wall joint than **18**. It can be used for horizontal boarding, but a tight fix at **x** should be avoided as it might hold water against the end grain of the board. A paintable width gap would be advantageous but could be obtained only if a very wide frame member were used. With a narrow gap, mastic pointing might be the answer but it would have to be well done.

In **20**, a tight fit at **x** is unlikely as the end board is very difficult to position.
A cover strip, **21**, is unfashionable but effective.
All these details would cause difficulties if used with lapped boarding but **19** is the most adaptable.

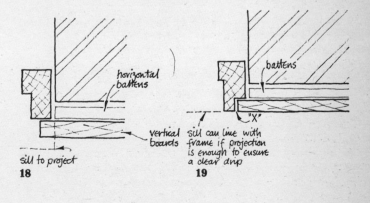

sill to project
18

sill can line with frame if projection is enough to ensure a clear drip
19

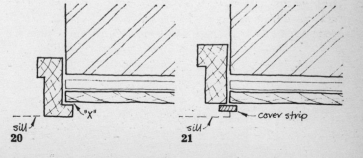

sill
20

sill
21

Head

Where the frame lines with front of battens, **18**, cladding can finish on the front of the frame, **22**.

The bottom edge should be chamfered. Any water that penetrates the cladding may be trapped and run back across the frame head. Full protection would mean using a flashing. A slight improvement to **22** would be to chamfer the edge of the frame, **23**, if its thickness allows and still leaves room for nailing.

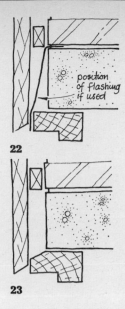

22

23

When the frame projects beyond the cladding, **20**, a flashed detail similar to **15** (with a flashing and breather membrane) for tiling can be used, but a cheaper alternative, **24**, may be suitable except on exposed sites.

In **24**, gap **x** should be wide enough to allow thorough painting of bottom edge of cladding (especially if boarding is vertical).

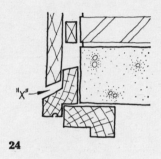

24

Sill

Whether an apron flashing is necessary depends upon:
1 exposure of site; 2 whether walling is of absorbent material; 3 how far the sill projects and whether it has good slope and drip.

If a flashing seems necessary it is better carried through and turned up the back of the sill, as shown in **6** for tile hanging.

A clipped-over sill, **25**, may be a reasonable compromise detail if the boards can be fixed.

25

For eaves and stop ends, conditions are similar to those for tile cladding but external corners need consideration. For vertical 'flat faced' boarding, method **26a** is sometimes used. The exposed end must be square edged. A tongued and grooved joint is unlikely to be possible on boards of normal thickness, so the joint will leak: this may be acceptable, depending upon the type of construction behind. A much better treatment is to finish on to a rebated corner member, **26b**.

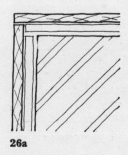

26a

26b

Timber cladding on timber frame

Details can be similar to those for timber on masonry but, as in tile cladding, some modifications may be possible because wood/wood joints are easier than wood/masonry.

Cost comparisons

Tile hanging or timber cladding allows a cheaper form of construction than cavity wall to be used, ie solid wall or timber frame. The cost of cheaper walling is therefore included in table I. Costs are for plain areas of tiling, not 'all in' costs, ie costs of cutting around openings, angle details, eaves details, etc. Cost of finishes alone (plus battens) is shown in table II. The indices are independent of table I, with machine-made sand-faced tiles taken as 100.

Tile hanging

The labour/material ratio of the cost of tile hanging (using average tiles) is approximately 50:50, so that the tile cost (which may range from £30 to £67 per 1000) can have a marked effect on the total.

Slate hanging

The cost of slate hanging (unless compared with best hand-made tiles) may be 10 to 15 per cent more than tile hanging. A wide variety of slate sizes is available. With reduction in size, the labour cost of slate hanging increases while material cost decreases.

Asbestos cement slates

These can be hung vertically 20 to 25 per cent more cheaply than natural Welsh slates.

Shingles too can be hung vertically but at a cost far in excess of tile or slate hanging.

Timber cladding

Most timber cladding boards have a maximum width of about 150 to 175 mm, which is related to the economics of converting logs into boards.

Vertical weatherboarding tends to cost more than horizontal boarding, owing to the cost of battening; eg 25 mm horizontal boards require fixing to battens at 1200 mm centres but 25 mm vertical boards must be fixed at 600 mm centres. Thicker boards require larger or more closely spaced battens. Although not shown in table I, tongued, grooved and v-jointed boarding will be slightly more expensive per m² of cladding than shiplap boarding because of the extra labour involved in forming the joints.

European redwood or western red cedar are probably the timbers most commonly used for external cladding. The latter costs about 2½ times as much as European redwood.

The difference in cost between ordinary redwood cladding and western red cedar boarding will be affected by maintenance cost. Cedar may be left untreated or be treated at intervals. Redwood might be painted, requiring fairly costly maintenance, or be treated with a coloured preservative which would involve lower maintenance expenditure.

The cost of both timber cladding and tile hanging may be affected by plugging battens to walls. If plugging can be avoided a saving can be made. Greater cost will be incurred if 'breather-type' building paper is specified as a 'second line of defence'.

Table I Cost comparisons of tile hanging and timber cladding on walling*

Inner wall	Outer skin	Cost per m²	Index
100 mm aerated concrete blocks + cavity	Brick facings (pc £20 per 1000)	£7·50–£10	100
100 mm concrete blocks + cavity	Brick facings (pc £50 per 1000)	£10–£13	125
9in (225 mm) brick commons	Machine-made sand-faced tiles on battens	£12–£15	152
225 mm brick commons	Hand-made sand-faced tiles on battens	£13·25–£16·50	166
225 mm brick commons	Plain concrete tiles on battens	£11·50–£14·75	151
140 mm lightweight concrete blocks	Machine-made sand-faced tiles on battens	£10–£11	106
Insulated timber stud wall with plywood sheathing	Machine-made sand-faced tiles on battens	£11·50–£12·50	118
Insulated timber stud wall with plywood sheathing	25 mm softwood matchboarding or shiplap boarding, painted	£10·35–£12·50	115
Insulated timber stud wall with plywood sheathing	25 mm western red cedar matchboarding or shiplap boarding	£12·50–£14·25	140

* Costs as at July 1974

Table II Cost of tiles and timber cladding*

Finish	Cost per m²	Index
Machine-made sand-faced tiles (Broseley or Staffordshire) on battens	£5·50–£6·00	100
Best hand-made sand-faced tiles on battens	£7·00–£7·50	124
Plain concrete tiles on battens	£5·25–£5·75	98
25 mm softwood matchboarding or shiplap boarding fixed vertically on battens	£4·50–£5·50	84
25 mm western red cedar boarding fixed vertically on battens	£6·50–£8·25	140

* Costs as at July 1974

Cost comparisons of flashing materials

After cost the main factors which determine the choice of a good flashing material are durability and flexibility. In spite of its high cost lead remains the material most widely used for flashing, in both roofing work and external walling. Cheaper alternatives exist but none has superseded lead in terms of durability, reliability and ease of use.

Today the prices of metals, particularly lead and zinc, tend to fluctuate almost daily, so it would be wise *always* to check prices or obtain quotations for specific jobs.

Table III gives basic prices of metals and materials suitable for flashing, with lead as 100 in the index.

Lead
Lead is the most suitable flashing material because it is the softest of the common metals and has very high ductility, malleability and corrosion resistance. Its low melting point makes it capable of being shaped with great ease with simple tools and it can easily be manipulated into complicated forms. The extreme durability of lead confirms its use as a flashing material. Its use entails no risk of staining to surrounding surfaces, and is vulnerable only to damp cement, oak and cedar. It is ideal for complicated site working, whereas copper and zinc cannot be pre-formed.

Copper
Copper is ductile and malleable and can be pressed or beaten into any shape without difficulty. It is widely used in spite of being second in cost only to lead. Like lead it can be formed to any required shape and will not become displaced. It may not always be suitable for flashings to external wall tiling because its green oxidation can cause green staining of the wall with which the metal is in contact.

Zinc
Zinc is cheaper than both lead and copper but is less durable and not so easily worked. Although zinc forms a protective film when exposed, atmospheric pollution causes it to weather away rapidly. Nevertheless in urban areas a life of 40 years can still be expected. Zinc possesses good working resistance to fatigue which enables it to be used for most flashing details. Zinc should *not* be fixed in direct contact with western timber claddings. Where it is used with walling materials containing soluble salts (notably chlorides and sulphates) the embedded portions need to be coated with bitumen.

Table III Cost comparisons of flashing materials*

Flashing	Basic price	Net price per m (150 mm wide)	Index
Milled lead (1·80 mm)	£368 per tonne	£1·18	100
Zinc (0·81 mm)	£33 per 50 kg	£0·59	50
Copper (0·56 mm)	£124·50 per 100 kg	£0·95	81
Aluminium (0·91 mm) commercial quality	£45·50 per 100 kg	£0·17	14
Nuralite	£3·94 per 2·40 × 0·90 m sheet	£0·27	23
Zincon	£6·16 per 10 m coil 150 mm wide	£0·61	52

* Costs as at July 1974

Aluminium
The relative price stability of aluminium compared with other metals has recently made it more economic. Aluminium is malleable, ductile and durable in normal conditions. Ease of working depends on composition. Commercial quality aluminium (99 per cent pure (IC)) is susceptible to work hardening. Super purity aluminium (99·99 per cent pure (I)) has greater ductility and is not susceptible to work hardening, but it costs over twice as much as normal quality (though less than the other metals considered). Intermediate grades are available—IB (99·5 per cent) and IA (99·8 per cent). The labour item involved in fixing aluminium flashings tends to be higher, so that the fixed cost of a super purity aluminium flashing comes close to that of an equivalent zinc flashing. The economics of this choice may then depend on the fluctuations in the price of zinc on the metal markets.

Aluminium sheet is liable to become corroded if in contact with wet western red cedar or Douglas fir. In polluted atmospheres it forms an oxide film which is not easy to clean off and which in time will turn into a matt black finish. In a rural atmosphere the surface will eventually acquire a smooth light grey tarnish.

Proprietary flashing materials
Nuralite is an asbestos/bitumen felt material which costs about the same as metals to fix. If acceptable it provides an economic alternative to metal flashings.

The price of Zincon strip (introduced in March 1972) is about half that of lead and, being soft, ductile, easy to cut and work, it costs the same to fix. Zincon has an Agrément certificate stating that the maintenance-free life will be at least 25 years, longer in non-industrial areas. Its scrap value is nominal and losses from site by theft are less likely than with lead.

Maintenance

With the exception of repointing every 20 to 25 years, brick-finished walls will be unlikely to incur any maintenance costs throughout their life. Most timber-clad walls require more periodic maintenance in the form of painting, varnishing or staining if their life is to be prolonged and their appearance retained (see AJ Handbook on the design and cleaning of windows and façades: Information sheet 2, table I, *The Architects' Journal*, 7 March 1973, pages 583-85). Tiled walls may be more susceptible to damage, eg through impact, than other finished walls and so may incur maintenance costs at some time. Replacing broken tiles and matching new with old causes problems.

10

Cavity wall lintels

Although the general requirements for cavity wall lintels are well known, faulty detailing or workmanship still occurs, **1**. If faults at this position cause rain penetration the trouble is usually very difficult to cure.

In addition to ensuring protection against rain penetration general points to be kept in mind include:

Appearance (especially 'ears' at each side of opening).

Effect of lintels upon thermal insulation (ie 'cold bridges').

Provision of adequate fixings for frames, blinds and curtains.

The need to consider suitable frame positions at lintels in relation to requirements at jambs (see detail 7, page 29) and sills (see detail 11, page 52).

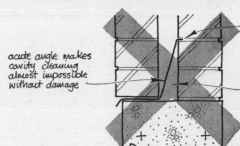

acute angle makes cavity cleaning almost impossible without damage

flashing not carried far enough into joint- 50mm recommended

void behind flashing means flashing material will be very vulnerable to damage, especially when cleaning the cavity

1

Avoidance of rain penetration

2 is better than **1** because:

Top of flashing carried 50 mm into internal walls is secure.

Cement and sand fillet behind flashing reduces chance of damage during cavity cleaning.

Weep holes help to drain or dry the cavity.

but the acute angle at bottom of cavity makes cleaning difficult.

In theory, **3** has the advantages of **2** and simplifies cleaning without damage but the flashing is unlikely to finish in the position shown unless it is both flexible and stuck down.

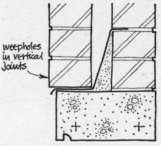

weepholes in vertical joints

2

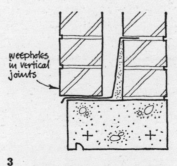

weepholes in vertical joints

3

With blockwork inner walls the normal (150 mm) rise of flashing will not reach the first blockwork joint, **4a**. Either increase the depth of flashing, **4b**, or start inner wall in brickwork or 150 mm course of blocks (usually available), **5**.

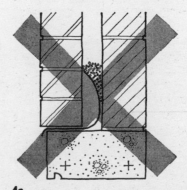

4a   **4b**

In **1** to **5** the flashing should project slightly beyond the lintel face but *not* beyond the brick face. Setting the lintel face back enables this to be done and provides a shadow which makes the flashing less noticeable. (The setback should be 15 to 25 mm, and not over a third of brick width as this is structurally risky.) Even with the projecting flashing there is some risk of water penetration across the top of the lintel. On exposed sites a boot lintel, **9**, would be better.

The single lintel right through the wall in **1** to **5** has a lower thermal insulation value than the cavity wall. The resulting 'cold bridge' may cause internal surface condensation. Such dampness may easily be confused with damp from a faulty flashing. Using a double lintel helps to reduce the cold bridge effect, especially if the inner lintel is of lightweight aggregate concrete.

BS 1239: 1956* describes the use of two lintels. The inner wall lintel has a chamfered nib to close the cavity, **6**. The problem of ensuring that the flashing finishes in the position shown is similar to **3** (ie it should be stuck down to rear lintel).

The flashing must project down in front of the window frame. If it does not, water may run back over the top of the frame.

If a double lintel system is used with window frame set forward and windows fixed *after* walling is complete, **7**, an appreciable length of flashing is left flapping until windows are positioned. Damage to this loose material is likely to occur and is difficult to remedy. This method should be used only when frames are 'built in' as the work proceeds. There is a risk of water penetration between flashing and window head unless the flashing is turned down and secured to the head.

With the introduction of thin prestressed concrete lintels there is some danger of the flashing being finished at the top of the inner lintel, **8a**. It *must* rise up the cavity the normal 150 mm, **8b**. Check specifications for this and check again during site supervision. **8a** also shows the outer lintel without any throating. This often happens when extra lintels need to be supplied quickly; they are made up on site, and the throating is omitted. Opinions differ about the value of lintel throatings. They are shown in BS 1239, and are essential on exposed sites or when the wall facing above is of an impervious type which results in considerable run-off of rain, but are advisable in all situations, **8b**.

Where a boot lintel is used the shape is frequently as **9**. This provides a good support for the flashing but, as in **2**, the acute angle at the bottom of the cavity makes cleaning out difficult.

* British Standards Institution, 2 Park Street, London W.1

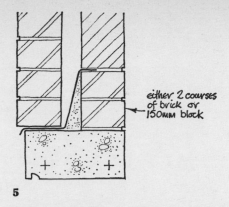

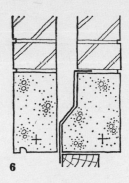

either 2 courses of brick or 150mm block

5

6

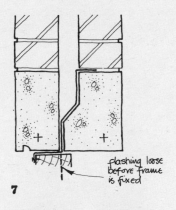

flashing loose before frame is fixed

7

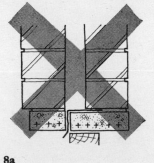

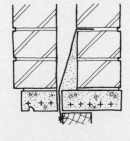

8a

8b

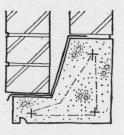

9

It is important that the end of the lintel flashing should throw water well clear of the vertical wall flashing, **10ab**, to prevent water crossing the cavity end. On site the need for this is not always realised.

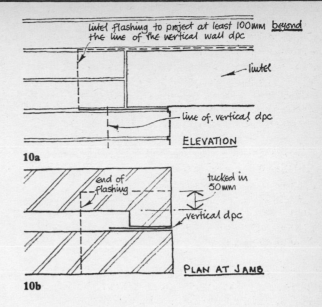

10a
lintel flashing to project at least 100mm _beyond_ the line of the vertical wall dpc

← lintel

line of. vertical dpc

ELEVATION

10b
end of flashing

tucked in 50mm

vertical dpc

PLAN AT JAMB

Lintel appearance

As flashings must be extended at the ends of lintels, and as they should always be bedded with mortar above and below, a thick joint may result which does not match with the normal jointing, **11**. A thick flashing material increases this effect. This occurs with all 'through-the-wall' lintels. With thin flashings and careful workmanship, a joint of normal width is possible. All lintels should have heights which are not a multiple of brick courses, eg a 'two-course' lintel should be two brick heights plus only one joint.

The 'ears' effect of exposed bearing ends is sometimes considered objectionable, **12**. With single 'through-the-wall' lintels and boot lintels, the ends can be cut back to allow cut bricks to go in front, or the nib of boot lintels can be cut back to allow whole bricks to be used, **13**.

With double lintels a cut-back end to the front lintel is not normally feasible as end bearing would reduce too much.

Thin brick slips are sometimes used to infill in front of cut-back lintel ends but are not easy to fix securely. A cut brick of at least 50 mm thickness is advised. Brick slips have occasionally been used as a facing across the full window width of concrete lintels. The risk of their coming loose and causing injury is considerable and this treatment is not advised with normal mortar fixing.

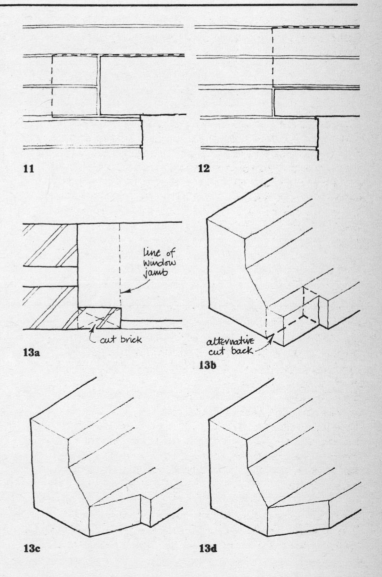

11

12

13a
line of window jamb

cut brick

13b
alternative cut back

13c

13d

If an all-brick effect is wanted, without using a brick arch, either a metal support, **14a** and **14b**, should be used or some form of reinforced brick lintel should be adopted, **15**. Reinforcing rods threaded through perforated bricks are probably the most satisfactory type (but this means using brick on end [soldier course] or brick on edge). Local authority acceptance of such methods should be confirmed before use.

With method **14b** there is considerable risk of water penetration between steel angle and window frame, unless the flashing is carried down and secured.

Architect **D. Rhodes** wrote: 'I was disappointed to notice that in Part 10 you perpetuate the detail of a steel angle supporting the external brick skin across an opening in a cavity wall. Such angles are structural steel members, and, since they lack any protection from weather and fire, they clearly do not comply with good practice or with by-laws, in the majority of buildings.

'District surveyors in the inner London boroughs have refused to accept this detail for many years, hence, no doubt, your caution regarding acceptance by local authorities. But surely acceptance by a building inspector is no automatic guarantee of safety, as recent events have brought home.'

Cecil Handisyde replied: 'Even though, as we said, local authority acceptance of such methods should be confirmed before use, these angles are made and used as lintels, and so must be found acceptable by many authorities.'

For long span windows, an alternative to the steel angle spanning full width of opening is to bolt it back at intervals to the inner rc lintel. Even if galvanised, as it should be, the angle still needs painting and, when painted, may appear much more intrusive on the job than it appeared on drawings. Some flashing materials would make satisfactory bedding of bricks difficult. A thin and very flexible flashing is needed.

If brickwork supported by the angle is to align with general walling, the bottom of the angle will be below normal mortar joint line and, at end bearings, will require bedding below, which further lowers the bottom of the bedding joint. The jamb brickwork can normally be cut to accommodate this, **16**, but the angle must be fixed *below* a course line and *not* bedded on a normal course. Failure to appreciate this results either in a botched appearance or omission of mortar bedding for bricks immediately above the angle (a most dangerous expedient).

Galvanised sheet steel lintels provide both support and protection against damp penetration and are an excellent alternative to the steel angle, **17**. They can be used with an rc or steel inner lintel. Also, being relatively thin, they cause fewer problems of thick joints or notched bricks.

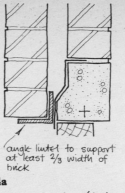

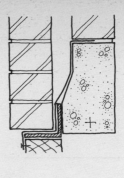

angle lintel to support at least 2/3 width of brick

14a

14b

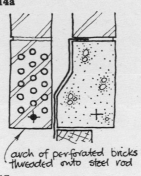

arch of perforated bricks threaded onto steel rod

15

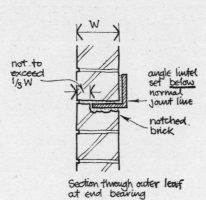

not to exceed 1/3 W

angle lintel set below normal joint line

notched brick

Section through outer leaf at end bearing

16

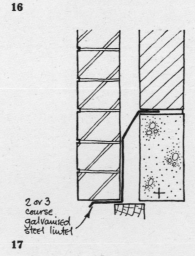

2 or 3 course galvanised steel lintel

17

Sometimes lintels are set with their front face slightly back from the general wall face. At end bearings, a small horizontal ledge of brick is exposed, **18**. At this point there is risk of damage by frost and sulphates, and the ledge should always be made up with cut brick facings.

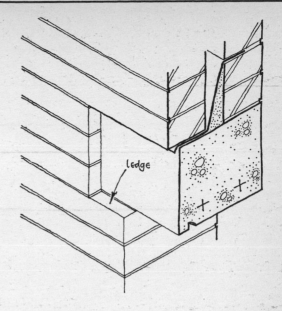

18

Fixings

BS 1239 includes provision for inserts in concrete lintels to provide fixings for window frames, curtain tracks, blinds, etc. It is not easy to predetermine all requirements precisely or to ensure that inserts are put in accurately. For this reason some people prefer to drill for fixings when positions can be accurately determined. If lintel inserts are to be used, lintel schedules should contain complete information. Timber inserts should not be placed close to corners or too close to reinforcement, **19**. Preferably they should not be used at all; there are many alternatives now available which do not shrink or rot.

With thin prestressed concrete lintels, fixing inserts are not practicable. Drilled fixings are also unlikely to be suitable and should not be made without checking that they will not weaken the lintel.

Steel lintels which support both outer and inner leaves of cavity walls may produce fixing problems in soffit positions, though shot-fixed or drilled and threaded fixings may be possible.

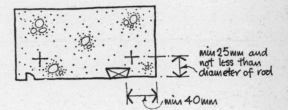

min 25mm and not less than diameter of rod

min 40mm

19

11

Window sills

Damp on inside of wall beneath window

Although detailing must prevent rain penetration, dampness is also caused by condensation running off glazing. With double glazing the risk is very small, but with single glazing trouble of this kind has increased, sometimes because of occupancy conditions but also because of the increasing use of draught-proof windows and the use of large areas of glazing. Where there is fairly continuous heating from a heat source immediately below the window, condensation may be quickly dispersed and cause little trouble, but in other cases single-glazed windows should have drained condensation channels.

1 has fixed glazing which is most vulnerable to condensation but a similar situation will occur on weatherproofed opening lights.

2 is better than **1** but water still lies in the drainage channel to some extent and damages painted wood before general repainting is needed.

A plastic or non-ferrous metal channel prevents damage. **3** is better than **1** or **2**, but as shown the section is difficult to clean.

A shallow and fairly wide channel is easier to clean, **4**. If used as shown the drainage tubes should run to lowest part of channel.

Condensation may accumulate on any horizontal members, such as transoms. Although not leading to wall dampness it will accelerate deterioration of materials. Condensation channels may not be needed but a sloping surface and, particularly, a sloping fillet to the glazing joint is advantageous.

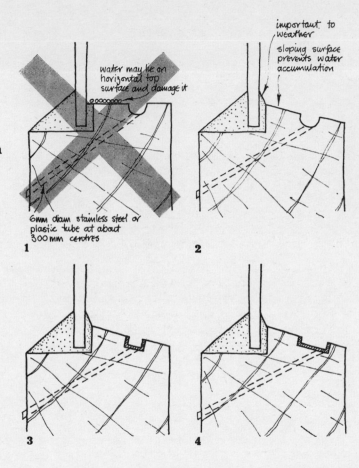

water may lie on horizontal top surface and damage it

6mm diam stainless steel or plastic tube at about 300mm centres

important to weather

sloping surface prevents water accumulation

1 2 3 4

Dampness and rain penetrating wall beneath sill

Assuming that the basic material of the sill is impervious damp penetration may occur:

Through sill to wall bed joint, **5**.

Through end of sill to wall jamb joint, **6**.

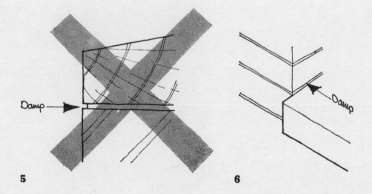

Damp

Damp

5 6

Through joints in length of sill, eg brick, **7,**

or joints in sills to long ranges of windows, **8.**

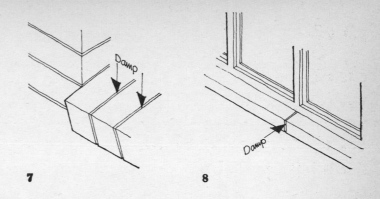

7   **8**

Sill to wall bed joint
Where sill projects far enough (ie 35-40 mm) and has good drip, **9, 10,** water penetration through the bed joint is rather unlikely.
Very severe exposure, eg coasts or some high buildings, may cause updraughts and more risk.

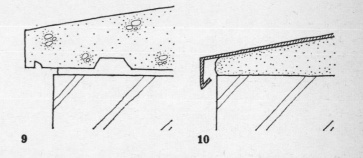

9   **10**

Sill to sub-sill joint
If the window is in a forward position, as in **16,** a sub-sill is unnecessary, but a window set back from the wall face may need a sub-sill, **11.** (In normal sections a wood sill should not exceed 175 mm width.)

Some movement between the wood sill and the sub-sill is likely, and the top surface of the sub-sill is very exposed both to direct rain and snow and to concentrated water run-off from glazing. So water penetration between sill and sub-sill is more likely than at bed joint between a projecting sill and wall below.

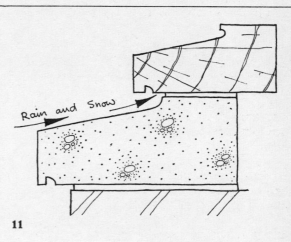

11

Traditional treatment is either a water bar, **12,** or a weather groove, **13.**

12 is feasible for built-in windows but may be difficult for windows fitted after walls are complete (unless there is enough tolerance to fit the window and its water bar into position).

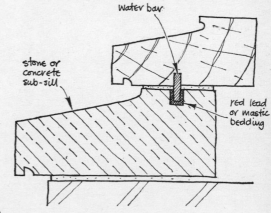

12

If the cavity wall is continued unbroken up to the underside of the sill, **13**, a weather groove on the underside of the sill may be adequate to check penetration *if* it is correctly positioned within the width of the cavity.

A sill as deep as **13** should have a second check just back from the face of the sash.

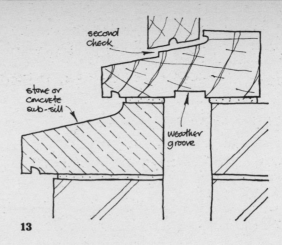

13

Jointed sills

With brick or other small unit sub-sill materials, joints form a weakness even if the basic material is impermeable.

Water is prevented from reaching the inner face either by a dpc, **14a**, or by taking the cavity up to the underside of the sill, **14bc**. In **14ab** the sub-sill, being flat and so exposed to frost, must be of special quality, whereas the sub-sill in **14c** is less vulnerable.

There is the disadvantage in **14a** of water lying on top of the flat brick sill, from where it may penetrate to the underside of the wood sill. Also the thin open joint between brick and front end of the wood sill is useless for access for painting the wood. In **14c** the mortar jointing should continue along the line of the brick slope and thus help to avoid water ingress.

A dpc beneath wood sills is still sometimes recommended even where water penetration is adequately prevented by cavity construction. Presumably the object is to safeguard the sill material from damage by contact with wet external walling. It is difficult to see why this sill condition is any worse than junctions between window frames and brick jambs where dpc protection is often not given. With hardwood or pressure-impregnated softwood sills the dpc seems a counsel of perfection except at the joint, **15, 16**.

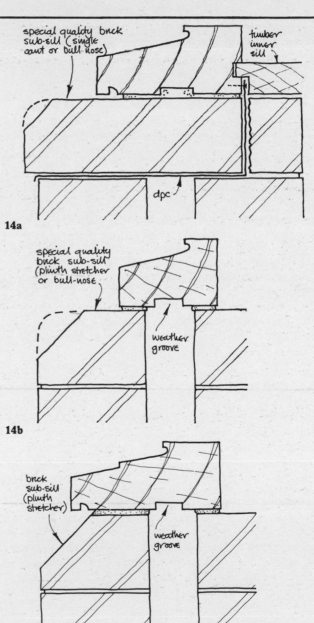

14a

14b

14c

Where long ranges of windows result in jointed sills, wood, plastic, metal or concrete, movement is bound to occur and adequate protection against damp penetration is essential, but quite often overlooked. A full length under-sill dpc is ideal. Failing this a good width of protection, say 200 mm each side of the joint, should be provided, **15**, and this dpc must be turned up behind the sill high enough to give full protection (**14a** shows timber inner sill and **16** shows tile sill).

Also the ends of timber sills must be treated against rot as end grain is vulnerable. The joint itself is best filled with non-hardening flexible mastic.

Long lengths of metal sills, especially aluminium, need expansion joints, otherwise they will buckle.

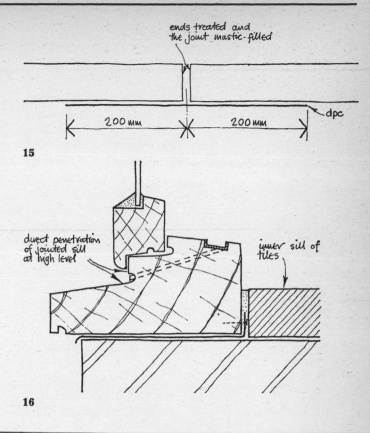

15

16

End of sill to wall joint
Old stone sills were usually built into the walls and jointing problems did not occur. Many hardwood sills also had projecting ends built-in, **17a**. Although some differential movement took place and damp walling was in contact with the sill, well-seasoned oak was very durable and serious damage rarely occurred. In the best work, projecting sills of stone or hardwood had stooled ends, **17b**.

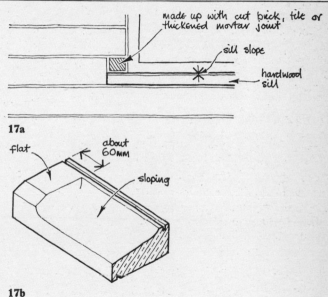

17a

17b

With softwood, damage often occurs if the sill end is built-in and it is now fairly common to detail the sill to stop short of the walling. The result is a joint between end of sill and wall into which water can easily penetrate, possibly reaching the wall interior and certainly reaching end grain of timber, **17c**.

A good mastic filling to the joint is the only feasible protection but the importance of this is not always appreciated. The requirement must be stressed and a careful site check is needed.
A softwood sill should in all cases be treated with preservative, under pressure or vacuum.

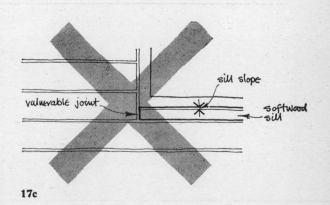

17c

External appearance of walling below sill

Disfigurement and sometimes damage, in walling immediately below sills, is common. Not all of this can be entirely avoided but careful detailing will minimise the trouble.

Sill projection

Sills collect a lot of run-off water from glazing and it is seldom sensible to design without a sill projection, **18**.

A projecting sill, with drip, throws most water clear (and helps to prevent water entry at the bed joint), but because it shelters the wall additional dirtying occurs immediately below.

Projection should be minimum possible consistent with providing a reasonable throw-off.

18

Stone and concrete require 25-35 mm sill projection, **19b**, but this depends upon accuracy of walling and care in placing the sill.

Timber requires about 25 mm, **19a**, but this also depends upon wall and workmanship.

Metal need be as little as 15 mm if wall is straight and workmanship good, **20a** (steel or aluminium), **20b** (zinc).

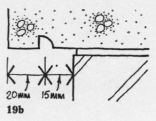

15mm 10mm
19a

20mm 15mm
19b

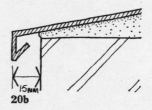

15mm
20a

15mm
20b

End of sill water run-off

Serious disfigurement often occurs from concentrated water run-off at the ends of the sills. Occasionally this shows as dark dirt streaking but more often as light colour streaking due to dirt being washed off the wall. Soluble limestone sills may result in considerable white streaking if the sill is incorrectly detailed, **21**.

21

Traditional stone sills usually had end stooling which prevented water blowing along and over the end of the sill, **22** and **17b**.

Continental zinc sill detailing provides a somewhat similar protection, **23**. If it is not built-in as walling proceeds, there may be a problem in matching the factory-made or pre-ordered sill with the actual structure size.

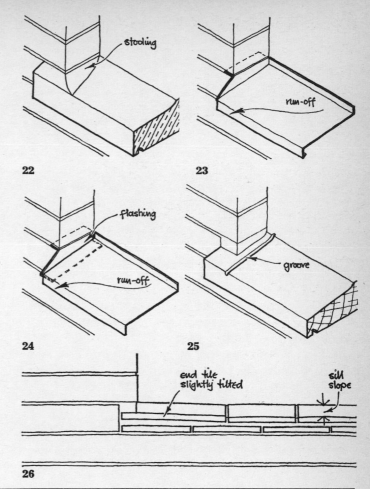

22   **23**

Aluminium and steel sills do not normally have any protection at the ends but a flashing may be used to provide a similar effect, **24**.

On wood sills a groove across the top of the sill may help to prevent much of the run-off by directing water to the front edge, **25**.

24   **25**

With tile, and possibly also with brick, sills the end units can be slightly tilted, **26**.

26

Proprietary sills
Proprietary slate sills can be used, **27**, but must have a dpc beneath if they are jointed on long ranges of windows.

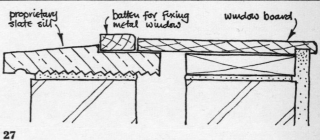

27

12

External doors: position of frame

The position of window frames in the thickness of walls usually depends on the appearance required, the external sill and internal window board size, and (in cavity walls) the need to relate frame position and vertical dpc. (See details 7, 10, 11, pages 29, 47 and 52 respectively.)
For external doors, threshold detailing may be a deciding factor (see detail 13, page 60). The effect of frame position upon the possible opening angle of the door can also be very important, especially for some outward opening doors.
For composite door/window units a compromise between conflicting requirements may be necessary; this means that designs for doors and windows must be considered together throughout the building.

Effect of frame position upon door swing
In **1**, the opening angle is limited by the wall, and in **2** by the architrave.

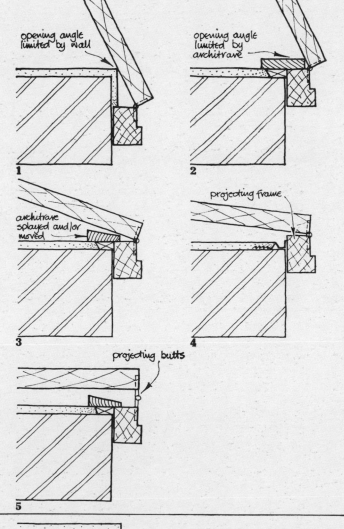

Architrave moved back and/or moulded, as in **3**, results in less restriction on opening angle.

Projecting frame as in **4** allows 180° opening but with a small frame secure fixing is not easy, and some form of joint, such as a metal plaster stop, is necessary to mask movement between plaster and frame.

Projecting butts, **5**, allow 180° opening including clearance of architraves. A stop may be needed to prevent the projecting handle from damaging the wall.

With inward opening doors the opening angle is not always critical but for many outward opening doors, eg to balconies or garden terraces, a 180° opening is very desirable to avoid obstruction and accidental damage by wind if the door is left unsecured.

Securing outward opening doors
With frame set back, **6**, wind can cause accidental damage at point of impact and strong levering action strains the butts, sometimes splitting wood at screw positions. With stout well-fixed butts the force may be transferred to the frame and loosen its fixing. The external door frame must be well fixed with lugs at about 450 mm centres.

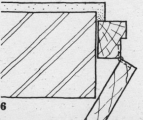

Overhead fixing devices are obtainable. Some are ugly and not all are robust enough for doors in windy positions. Cabin hooks may not be ideally convenient but they are relatively inexpensive and give a secure fixing.

180° opening allows a small cabin hook near outer end of the door, **7**.

Restricted opening angle, as in **8**, means a short cabin hook **a** must be towards hinge end of door, which is inconvenient and not always efficient in strong winds. Alternatively a very long hook, **b**, can be used.

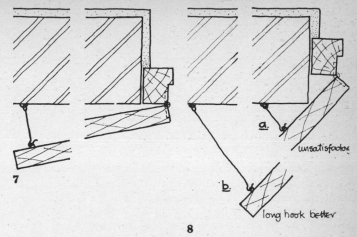

Where doors cannot open much beyond 90°, a post is often added as an afterthought, **9**, and can be a hazard when the door is shut.

A better arrangement is to form either a solid barrier, **10**, or at least an easily seen check.

It is better that cabin hooks should be fixed to the *wall* than to the door. Builders seem to do the opposite unless specially instructed. Hooks swing in the wind and usually do less damage to the wall than to door finishes.

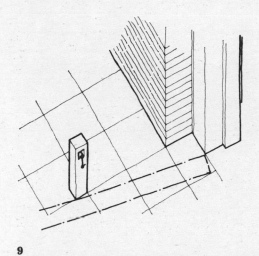

9

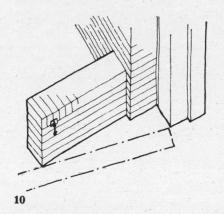

10

Relation of door frame position to wall dpc in cavity
Door set back in wall, **11**, allows reasonable opening angle, but frame does not cover inner wall material. Water may enter and material may be unacceptable in appearance. In **12** the dpc is covered with an external lining. This must be rot-protected or of non-corrodable metal.

If the door frame is fixed towards the outer face of the wall, **13**, the dpc and inner wall material are covered satisfactorily. This restricts the opening angle of the door, and if an external step is required, the step will project more than in position **11** and **12**.

Effect of threshold upon frame position
Threshold detailing is described in detail 13 (page 60), but note that a step at door position often determines threshold position, which in turn decides the frame position.

R. Hadap from Ayrshire drew attention to figures **11**, **12** and **13** showing relation of door frame position to wall vertical dpc in the cavity. To avoid an exposed dpc, **11**, and/or additional lining to cover it, **12**, without changing the position of the door frame, **13**, he suggested that the door opening can be formed in the cavity wall using cut bricks or special bricks as shown in his sketch (right).

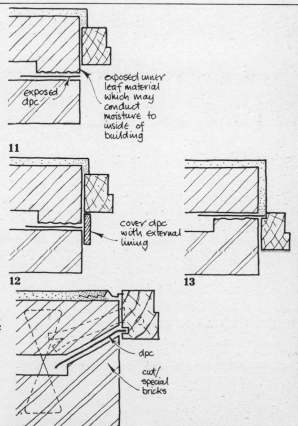

Hadap's solution.

13

External doors: thresholds

Failures of external door thresholds often occur because traditional details are used for unusual or changing conditions, such as the following:

an increasing requirement for unobstructed access (ie a level platform outside the door and no upstand threshold);

an increasing demand for effective draught exclusion;

doorways to exposed upper floor balconies where the threshold must prevent not only rain penetration to the floor at that level, but also leakage beneath, affecting rooms below;

increased use of types of internal floor finish which are particularly vulnerable to damage if water reaches the fixing adhesive.

Design check list

In order that reasonable detailing may later be possible consider the factors below.

Severity of site exposure

Is porch or lobby protection
  possible?
  essential?
  desirable?
  unimportant?

Is unobstructed entry (ie no step, no threshold upstand)
  required by regulations?
  desirable?
  unimportant?

Is door inward or outward opening?

If there is a step up to inside floor, where should the riser be for
  safety?
  convenience?
  assisting water exclusion?

Will cross falls on external paving cause problems (eg as on some access balconies)?

Where in the walling thickness can the door frame be (ie in relation to vertical wall dpc)? Threshold related to a step may affect this.

Is it an upper floor access with special need to guard against damage to rooms below from water entry *beneath* the threshold?

Is internal floor finish, especially the vulnerable adhesive fixed type, immediately inside the doorway?

Is a matwell or mat on top of floor required?

Does doorway interrupt normal horizontal wall dpc? If so, what treatment is required?

Threshold details

Weatherboard
Traditional weatherboard is shown in **1a, c,** but alternative **1b** is more economical in use of timber.

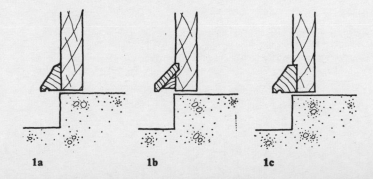

1a   1b   1c

Inward opening doors: total water exclusion not essential

For some types of room, eg stores or wall enclosed outdoor spaces, it may be very convenient to be able to brush or wash out through the doorway. Any form of upstand obstruction must then be avoided.

Rain exclusion is obviously assisted in such cases if room use permits a step at the entrance, **1, 3a**.
For similar conditions but where a step cannot be used some rain entry, in driving wind, will occur.

A short sharp ramp from door outward, **2a**, may keep out water in most weather, but in bad conditions penetration may take place and the flat inside floor will allow water to lie.

If the floor is at all uneven the water may spread inward.

The ramp could be continued inward, **2b**, but an inward opening closed door will have a gap at the bottom to allow clearance when it opens. Rising butts will reduce this gap.

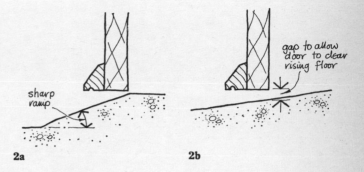

2a **2b**

Outward opening doors

It is possible to put the step in **1** behind the door, as in **3a**.
With a ramp, as **2b**, an outward opening door will need no clearance gap below, **3b**.

In **1-3**, draught exclusion is assumed to be unimportant. Where it does matter, a rising draught excluder fixed to the door is probably the best answer.

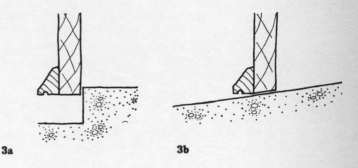

3a **3b**

Metal weatherbar threshold

A detail of the type in **4** is sometimes used in an effort to provide an 'unobstructed' entry, but it forms a nasty hazard and is especially dangerous for use in positions when the door may sometimes be fixed open. It will keep out rain in moderate exposures but is not proof against driving rain or snow. It may also be unsatisfactory because rain driving into the space between door and frame runs down the rebate and reaches the floor *inside* the end of the weather bar. A vulnerable floor finish immediately inside the door is inadvisable.

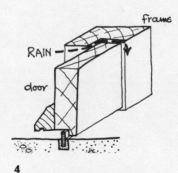

4

A better alternative might be to use a compressible type draught excluder let into the floor, **5**.
This is a less hazardous obstruction than the weatherbar of **4** and if well fitted can prove reasonably watertight in moderate exposure, but has some of the same disadvantages as **4**.

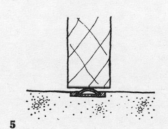

5

Inward opening door: wood threshold plus step

A detail such as **6** is commonly used. In exposed conditions some rain or snow may be blown in, and the addition of a drained internal channel should be considered, **7**.

If the door is thick, about 40 mm or more, an improvement to **6** and **7** is possible by rebating the bottom of the door enough to allow the weather mould to drip clear of a small threshold, **8**, but if this threshold also has a drop, it may be difficult to fix. An extended threshold, going beyond the internal face of the door, may then be needed.

When bottom of door is rebated it may be impossible to fix flush bolts.

In **6, 7, 8a**, the threshold is rebated so that the door stops against it. This helps to keep out draught but serves very little purpose against rain penetration. A flat-topped threshold with inset draught excluder may be equally or more effective, **8b**.

R. E. Owen, referring to methods **6** and **7** suggested using an upstanding galvanised w.i. water bar in the door sill, covered by a throated rebate in the bottom edge of the door (*see section and plan, right*). With external inward opening flush doors wind-blown rain spreads laterally into the rebate, and a throat in the joint rebate is essential to carry this water to the outer face of the water bar at the bottom. The top edge of the weatherboard should weather steeply and be waterproof-glued and screwed to the door face (tonguing in allows water to enter the cut edges of the ply face in the corresponding groove in the door). The upstanding metal 'blade' of a water bar or its equivalent is an almost invaluable device for forming inward and outward facing rebates with negligible horizontal top surface. Such bars and channels are widely used in continental inward opening window and door details. The external door detail described is based upon experience of some 1000 houses in all exposures.

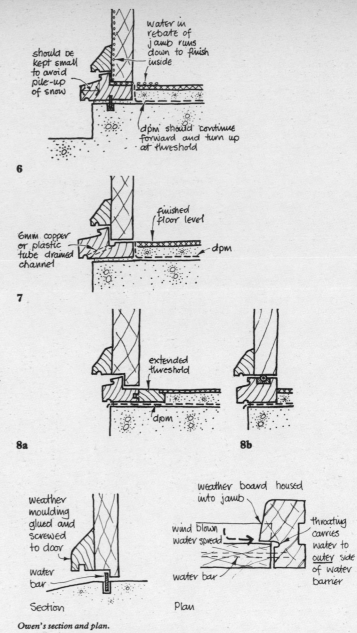

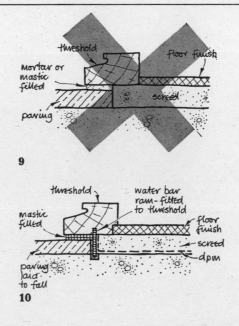

Owen's section and plan.

Water penetration beneath threshold

Although not immediately obvious, water getting in beneath a threshold may reach the edge or underside of vulnerable floor finishes.

Trouble of this kind is unlikely when a wood threshold occurs at a step, but details similar to **9** are sometimes seen and would not be satisfactory—even with a mastic bedding.

A waterbar, **10,** is the traditional method of protection in such cases and should be adequate at ground floor doors but is not a complete answer to the upper floor situation where protection to a room below is needed.

Upper floor problems

When an upper floor external doorway has to provide against any risk of water penetration to rooms below, a number of problems arise.

Exposure conditions are often more severe than at ground level.

Drainage falls on the balcony may produce unforeseen complications.

The waterproof finish to the balcony is sometimes shown extending to a position beneath the threshold where proper workmanship becomes impossible.

An adequate upstand to the balcony waterproofing may result in the need for stepped floor construction which produces structural problems, and which must therefore be solved at early design stage.

11 does not allow for probable variations in level of balcony finish such as occur on long access balconies. Also the asphalt-to-water bar joint is by no means certain to be effective.

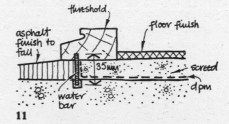

11

In **12,** asphalt is shown with turn-up into grooved threshold, but in practice the material cannot be properly worked into position as groove is too far back and height insufficient.

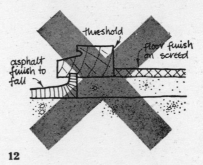

12

The asphalt in **13** could be worked into position, but in practice the balcony falls may turn out to leave the asphalt skirting lower than expected. The architect should anticipate falls and allow for them.

Even as shown there is a step in the concrete which must have been accepted at design stage.

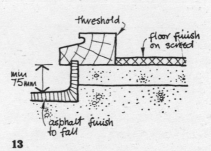

13

Except in very sheltered situations it is difficult to see how to provide a satisfactory detail without some form of structural upstand beneath the threshold. If a step in the concrete slab is not acceptable structurally, then it may be necessary to provide a concrete upstand, **14**, in spite of its nuisance value in making access less easy. The upstand should be high enough to be noticeable, to prevent people tripping over it.

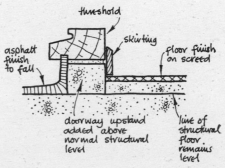

14

A possible method would be to use lead flashing, **15**. The flashing must be fixed to the wood thresholds and later dressed into asphalt. There is risk of damage to the front lead in the interim period.

If the balcony runs above a lower floor room and requires thermal insulation on top of the structural material, the problems of balcony finish level and internal floor level are further increased. Structure and detail are interdependent. It is not safe to 'leave the details till later on'.

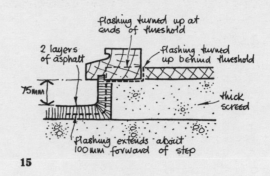

15

Where upper floor construction is of timber the problems are basically the same but with the additional hazard of more structural movement. A substantial step-up in the structure becomes more imperative. A cover flashing coming over and down the outside of the asphalt should be provided, **16**. This is the most sensible type of detail for balconies.

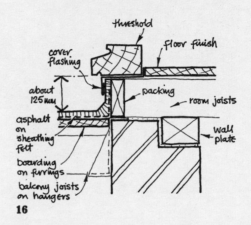

16

Outward opening doors
The door/threshold detail is clearly easier but prevention of water leakage between threshold and structure remains similar to the examples illustrated.

Relationship of wall/floor dpc
Depending upon relationship of wall dpc and ground floor damp proof membrane, problems of continuity of protection will occur. On sloping sites conditions may vary at different doorways and a 'standard detail' may not meet all requirements. Each case needs special consideration, but a point easily overlooked is that it is usually necessary to extend the floor dpm into the door frame, **17**.

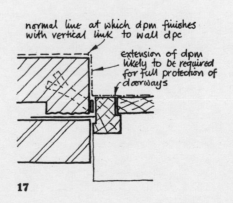

17

14

Masonry walls: junction of timber upper floors

Plaster faults

Two faults which frequently occur in present-day building are:

1 cracking of plaster;

2 uneven line at junction of wall and ceiling plaster. This is not always easily seen at construction stage but may become painfully obvious after decoration, especially when wall and ceiling decorations are not similar in material and/or colour.

At the end of the contract 'defects' period clients want the faults corrected. Is it fair to blame the contractor? Poor workmanship or materials may be partially the cause, but architects too have, over a period of time, accepted a number of changes in design and construction that, in combination, cannot be expected to be trouble free, **1, 2**.

Traditional construction

Heavy cornice prevents cracking at junction and disguises uneven ceiling. Good 'break-line' for decorations, **1a**.

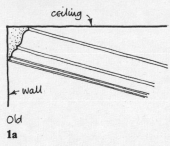

Old
1a

Floor joists generous in size and closely spaced.

Timber well seasoned.

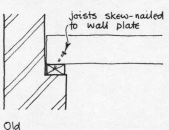

Old
2a

Joists securely fixed to wall plates, **2a**.

Thick lath and plaster ceiling is relatively strong and can readily be used to take up any differences in levels of underside of joists and thus make a level ceiling/wall junction possible.

New construction

No cornice causes weak junction; uneven ceiling line shows up; no decoration 'break-line', **1b**.

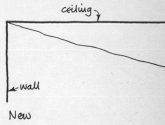

New
1b

Economy in timber; small joists, wider spaced; deflection and movement more likely.

Poorly seasoned timber; more movement resulting from central heating.

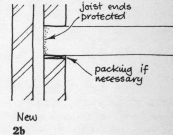

New
2b

Joists loosely fixed to wall, often unsecured and quite frequently 'levelled' by wedging up with any odd bits of material that happen to be nearby, **2b**.

Thin plasterboard has to *follow* ceiling joist levels. Thin plaster skim coat insufficient to allow making up uneven levels. Insufficient strength at plasterboard joints to prevent cracking caused by movement in timber.

There does not appear to be any cheap or simple means of overcoming these problems. Noggings between joists around the perimeter of the room add some stiffness and can be set out to provide a level starting line for ceiling boards, **3** (view of underside of ceiling).
Some irregularity of the ceiling away from the wall would still exist but would be less noticeable than at the wall position.

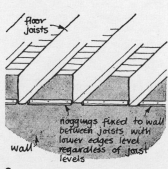

3

A method sometimes tried is to form a trowel cut to prevent any bond between ceiling and wall plaster. If carried out properly this may restrict the cracking to that line. It does nothing to help on levelling.

Adding a small wood moulding or preformed cornice has been tried, **4**. This may hide plaster cracks but will usually result in a crack between plaster and wood because of shrinkage. It does provide a useful edge on which to change decoration but is likely to emphasise any unevenness in the ceiling.

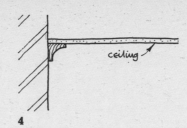

4

Joist deterioration

Although it is now accepted that wood wall plates should *not* be built into walls, joist ends are normally carried into the inner leaf of cavity walling and exposed to cavity conditions. All too often this method seems to be used without taking any precaution against timber decay. Ideally joists should be pressure treated with preservative but, failing this, at least joist ends should be protected, either by wrapping in a waterproof material or by liberal treatment of brush-applied preservative.

A possible alternative to building-in is to carry joists on joist hangers (see **5**).

Effect of floor upon wall stability

With low rise buildings and small floor spans, wall stability often may not be a critical factor but it should not be ignored. A combination of design changes may lead to conditions which would seldom have occurred in the past.

The use of joist hangers which may lead to more eccentric loading, the use of thin concrete block walls, larger windows and the trend towards eliminating 'structural' internal partitions may add up to produce construction of questionable safety or even positive overloading. The following points should be considered.

Floors supported on hangers
On some small jobs where continuity of work for bricklayers may not be available elsewhere on the site, hangers avoid a hold up for bricklayers while joists are fixed, but they may have an effect on wall stability, and there must be some means of preventing hangers from pulling out of the wall if shrinkage occurs.

If the joist is not well secured, ie with at least two nails, the floor load should be considered as acting at the inner face of the wall, **5ab**.

5a with one-nail fixing has a fully eccentric load. In **5b**, with two-nail fixing, the eccentricity is taken as d/2 (usually 25 mm).

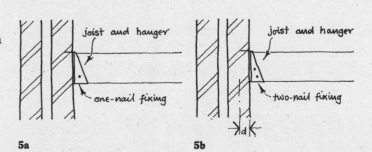

5a **5b**

Hangers can be inserted as the walling proceeds but it is important, because of the added eccentricity, that joists should not be fixed *and loaded* before walling has had time to gain reasonable strength. This is most likely to be important in cold weather conditions when carpenters might continue to work but mortar would be slow to acquire strength.

It may be thought that joist hangers have an advantage in that the walling is not interrupted, as it is when joists are built in. This depends very much upon how the space between joists is filled. Good infilling is more difficult with blocks than with smaller brick size units (unless joists are spaced to accept one standard block between each).

Where walling is designed to CP 111, Part 2, 1970,* positive support from intermediate floors is often required. The code gives examples of how to achieve this, **6ab**. For cavity walls the illustrated methods seem to have possible snags, **7ab**.

In **7b**, because straps are 6 mm thick they need pre-drilling. The result may be that the turndown of strap is loose in the cavity.

Also, unless the joist is packed to the wall, the wall is able to move inward.
Since under the code bracing is required only at 1·2 m or 1·8 m intervals, a single bad fit would leave the wall unsupported for 2·4 m or 3·6 m.

Matthew A. Berwick of Leslie, Fife, provided details, **8, 9**, of accepted Scottish practice, from the *Explanatory memorandum* referring to the structural strength requirements of the Building Standards (Scotland) Regulations. He pointed out that in each case the anchors extend through the cavity to the outer leaf, thereby effectively spreading any load over both leaves of the wall as well as improving stability of the outer leaf. The difficulties referred to above could thereby be largely avoided.

A similar construction is used to anchor the roof structure to gable walls.

A. Hickman wrote: 'With reference to detail 14, I would suggest:
1 use thicknessed joists and supervise lining through (if this fails, cross-batten undersides of joists, wedging as necessary to give a true line, and fix plasterboard to battens);
2 ensure that the joists specified and used are of adequate width to provide a secure fixing for the ends of plasterboard;
3 ensure that solid blocking or herringbone strutting is fixed not more than 100 mm from joist ends at the time the joists are placed to prevent twisting;
4 use correct thickness of plasterboard for joist spacings;
5 stack plasterboard flat on site in a reasonably dry atmosphere;
6 use plasterboard cove cornice.'

*British Standards Institution, 2 Park Street, London W.1

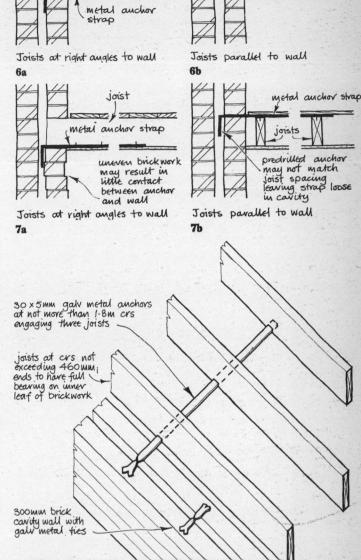

Joists at right angles to wall
6a

Joists parallel to wall
6b

Joists at right angles to wall
7a

Joists parallel to wall
7b

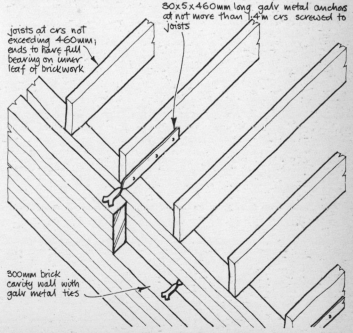

8 *Joists parallel to wall and flooring nailed to joists.*

9 *Joists at right angles to wall.*

15

Masonry walls: junction with concrete upper floors

Based upon BS CP 3: Part 2: 1970,* calculated loadbearing masonry walls of normal cavity type often provide an economic structure, especially for domestic or similar buildings with short floor spans. Intermediate upper floors of concrete may be required, and sometimes these may extend through to the exterior face of the walling, or at least part-way through to support upper walling.

This section does *not* consider the structural aspects but

* British Standards Institution, 2 Park Street, London W.1

illustrates three points of detailing:
1 preventing damp penetration;
2 the use of brick 'tiles';
3 the 'cold bridge' effect resulting from loss of cavity insulation value.

Very similar points of detail would apply if the construction included a ring beam, but as a beam is often deeper than floor thickness the problem of safely securing thin brick tiles might be greater.

Preventing damp penetration

The most obvious need is for an effective cavity flashing above the concrete floor.

The flashing material can project and be folded down, **1**. This is poor in appearance and the fold-down is seldom achieved in practice.

If it is kept back from the wall face and the joint pointed up, settlement due to compression of the flashing may concentrate the load and cause spalling, **2a**.

The preferable method is to insert a preformed metal drip section, **2b**.

Although structural design is not being discussed here, the type of flashing material may have structural implications. If compressible it will affect load transfer down the walling and may cause most or all of the load to be carried on the inner leaf. It will also affect the bond of the outer leaf to its support and so reduce ability of the walling to resist wind forces. This may be important on exposed sites and especially so in the top storey of a building where wind causes negative pressure and tends to lift the roof off the top of the wall (see detail 17, page 76).

Robert Toy, of Falmouth, Cornwall, suggested that the 'solid backing to support flashing' in **2b** is impractical. 'If the flashing is of non-rigid material and does cross the cavity at an angle (as **2b** and 99 per cent of similar details drawn in architects' offices indicate), then the flashing would indeed need a backing to prevent it being damaged when the cavity is cleaned out, but such a backing would be difficult and therefore expensive to install.

'A more practical detail is to carry the flashing vertically down the outer face of the inner leaf to slab level and then across the width of the cavity and under the outer leaf to the outside face.

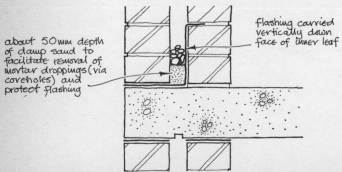

about 50mm depth of damp sand to facilitate removal of mortar droppings (via coreholes) and protect flashing

flashing carried vertically down face of inner leaf

Toy's suggestion.

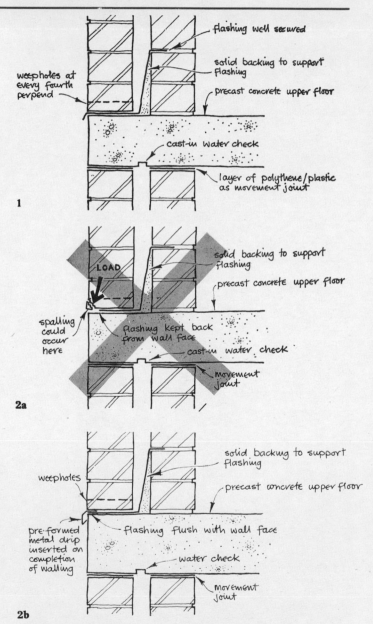

1

flashing well secured

solid backing to support flashing

precast concrete upper floor

weepholes at every fourth perpend

cast-in water check

layer of polythene/plastic as movement joint

2a

LOAD

solid backing to support flashing

precast concrete upper floor

spalling could occur here

flashing kept back from wall face

cast-in water check

movement joint

2b

solid backing to support flashing

precast concrete upper floor

weepholes

pre-formed metal drip inserted on completion of walling

flashing flush with wall face

water check

movement joint

'If the bottom of the cavity is filled with damp sand to a depth of approximately 50 mm while the wall is being built, then the accumulation of mortar droppings which inevitably occurs can easily be broken up with the end of a lath in the traditional manner and cleared out with the sand via core-holes, leaving the bottom of the cavity perfectly clean and the flashing undamaged.'

Cecil Handisyde replied: 'This proposal is a good one, if there is supervision which ensures that cavities are cleaned out. All too often this process seems to be omitted; 50 mm of sand would then add to the height of the pile-up of mortar droppings.'

Comments from **John Duell,** of London: 'The "z" shape in **2b** is difficult to achieve on site with the materials most used today, pitch polymer and polythene. Haunching is costly and rarely done today. The "z" shape makes the geometry of corners and junctions difficult. I would suggest an "L"-shaped dp tray which requires no haunching and which gives a simple geometry at corners. It also allows for easier cleaning of mortar droppings from the dpc.
'The projection of a dpc is indeed difficult to obtain on site. I recently interviewed most of the architects of recent large loadbearing brickwork projects and only in one or two cases was an attempt made to project the dpc. I would suggest the dpc is brought just to the face. (Incidentally, the metal drip in figure **2b** should be tucked *under* the dpc, not over it, and it would cost a fortune.)

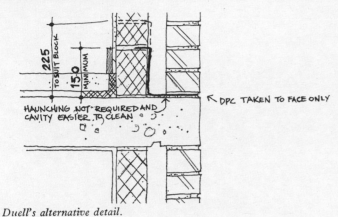

Duell's alternative detail.

'Mention should be made that laps need to be sealed by a method suitable for the material used. (This is particularly difficult with polythene.)
'Consideration should be given to the formation of corners and junctions which has been traditionally left to the bricklayer's expertise and few architects in my survey were aware of how junctions were formed. With today's standard of workmanship and with the increased exposure of medium and high rise buildings this reliance may not be sufficient. (Pre-formed corners are available from some manufacturers or may be made up in a site hut.)
'The above discussion outlines the fact that the detailing and installation of stepped dpcs (cf horizontal dpcs) is not properly covered in textbooks, British Standards, BRS documents, etc.'

Cecil Handisyde replied: 'Unless either stuck into position with adhesive or provided as pre-formed stiff material, the "L"-shaped dpc is likely, in practice, to finish up more like that of the original detail. Mr Duell's other comments are a very useful contribution.'

Water penetration *below* the floor slab is often not considered but there is a possibility of movement causing cracking at the junction of wall and slab. Some form of drip over the cavity is therefore advisable to prevent water reaching the inner leaf. **2** shows drip formed in concrete, which is feasible in a framed building with concrete cast first and brickwork built up to it later. If the concrete is cast in situ the top of the cavity must be closed in some way in any case, and a T-section or channel in plastic or rust resistant metal can serve both functions, **3ab**.

Alternatively, if visually acceptable, the concrete may project beyond the wall but shuttering then becomes more complicated. The projection may also form a catchment for water, which may penetrate beneath the cavity flashing. It should either be weathered, **4a**, or, better, stepped, **4b**.

Flashing could have preformed drip as **2b**.

Robert Rogerson and **Philip Spence** of Glasgow commented that damp-proofing procedures in the West of Scotland need to be quite different to those in any other part of the country. They consider that in those conditions a concrete slab going through to the exterior of a wall, even with protection above, is not satisfactory. They advised that the outer brick leaf of the cavity wall should pass uninterrupted past any slab, and that there should be a dpc between the external wall and the slab.

Cecil Handisyde replied: 'This is a most useful reminder that special local site conditions need to be considered. The West of Scotland is, indeed, not the only area where "normal" methods would be unsatisfactory. Trouble is known

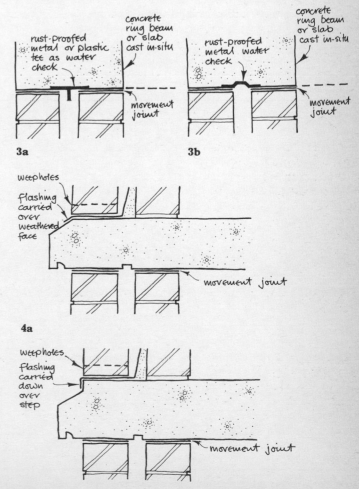

to have occurred on exposed coastal sites in South and South-West England. It should be noted that in any but small domestic buildings Robert Rogerson and Philip

Spence's solution to dampness may have structural implications in terms of wall design.'

The use of brick 'tiles'

One fairly common arrangement is to stop the concrete behind the wall face to allow the face brickwork to be carried past as brick 'tiles'. Detailing becomes critical because the concrete must project to not less than two-thirds of the outer wall thickness. Experience shows that in some districts building surveyors will be very strict on this; for example they will measure the width of bricks as used. The result is to leave very little space for brick 'tiles' and their fixing—it could be as little as 33 mm, **5**.

Allowing 8 or 9 mm for bedding between tiles and concrete, the tile thickness cannot be more than about 24 mm. With clay bricks it is better to machine cut the bricks for the purpose than to try to obtain 'specials' which, even if available, might well vary in colour from the general brickwork.

Safe fixing for the brick 'tiles' is not easy to achieve. If any load is transferred to them from the wall above there is a risk of 'bowing' under compression, **6**. In concrete frame structures this problem requires special precautions, as differential movement of frame and wall causes difficulties.* In such cases the outer brick walls are not structural and an expansion joint at the top of the wall may be needed to take up differential movement between wall and column.

The risk of 'bowing' will increase as the height of brick tiling increases.

There is some doubt about what type of material should be used for fixing the tiles. At the present time careful work using ordinary mortar is probably the best choice.

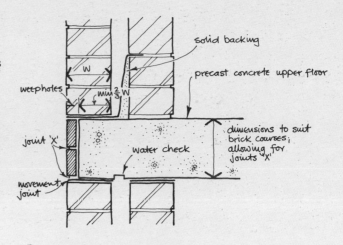

5

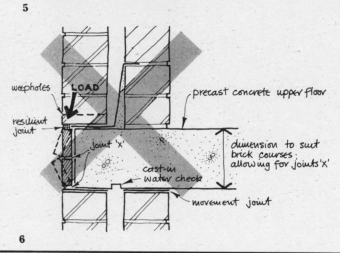

6

The 'cold bridge' effect

The risks of cold bridges leading to internal condensation are now fairly well appreciated, but perhaps are more often thought of in terms of panel wall type construction than where floors cause a bridge where they cross a cavity wall.

Whether a through-the-wall floor will be a serious risk can be judged only for particular situations and it will depend upon humidity, ventilation and heating conditions of the adjacent rooms.
If the situation seems to call for precautions the lost cavity insulation value should be replaced by adding insulation inside. The risk of condensation can be reduced by using a 'closed cell' plastic or polyurethane insulant, sealed with pvc tape at joints.

Ceiling insulation may be applied to the underside of the concrete, **7**, but this may result in a visually unsatisfactory drop in ceiling level for the width of the insulation. If a ceiling finish is fixed to battens the extra insulation can be located within the batten depth airspace.

Alternatively insulation can be inset into the slab thickness, but this may involve an additional bend to reinforcement even where otherwise structurally acceptable.

* For discussion and treatment see Brick Development Association Technical Note *Some observations on the design of brickwork cladding to multi-storey rc framed structures*, Vol I, No 4, September 1971

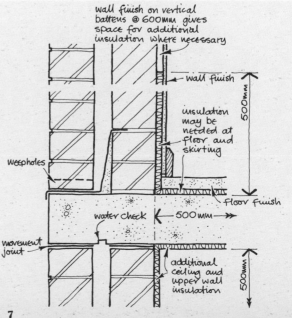

7

There may be a need for floor insulation. If so, the floor finish must be able to accommodate the thickness.

In high risk situations, wall insulation above and below the slab thickness may be needed. Again, accommodating the thickness can be awkward unless a wall finish on battens is used.

J. H. Pickwick commented: 'The junction of masonry walls with upper concrete floors involves three particular precautions:

1 Vertical shrinkage and creep dictates that the movement joint shown at the top of the masonry panels should be 12-15 mm and be of compressible filler (pointed with a compressible sealant) rather than a thin membrane.
2 The introduction of a movement or pressure relieving joint necessitates that a metal anchor be cast into the slab and built into the brickwork below to provide lateral resistance to wind forces. Such an anchor should not provide a bridge for water across the cavity and ideally should at the same time allow vertical movement of the masonry.

3 Where brick tiles are introduced into this situation they will require additional means of support to the conventional mortars. Figures 6 to 8 of the BDA Technical Note* show two alternative methods of supporting the metal tiles using metal straps, plates and anchors, or the tiles can be bedded with adhesives.'

Cecil Handisyde replied:
'1 I agree the movement joint needs to be 12-15 mm if the structure is a framed concrete one. I very much doubt the need for this in small buildings where a concrete intermediate floor bears on brick walls; and unless the bearing is on to cross walls a separation would not be possible.
2 In framed buildings where a full movement joint is necessary it is not always essential to have a top fixing with metal anchors. The need depends upon panel wall size and shape. In some cases, end fixings to columns may be adequate.
3 The fixing of brick slips is a difficult problem on which BDA Technical Note 4* is useful. Metal fixings may be the best method but improvements in adhesives may be sufficient to give satisfactory performance.'

* See reference on page 70

16

Low buildings against higher cavity walls

Although properly built cavity construction prevents rain penetration reaching the inner wall, a considerable amount of water may enter the outer leaf and some may run down its inside face. This is well understood, and usually no trouble occurs if a proper cavity cloak is provided at all points where the cavity is bridged horizontally, and if at the bottom of the wall the cavity extends well below dpc (see detail 5, page 20).

But things may go wrong when a low building abuts a higher cavity wall. Unless preventive measures are taken, water penetrating the exposed high-level outer skin of the cavity and running down its inside face wets what at a lower level is an interior wall, **1**.

If both high and low building are designed at the same time this possibility is likely to be foreseen and overcome by a cavity cloak just above low roof level. When the low building is added later as an extension there is more chance of the problem being overlooked. There is also much greater difficulty in forming the necessary protection to the existing external wall, which becomes the internal wall of the new extension.

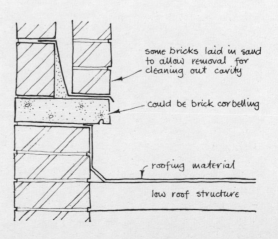

1

Both levels built at same time

Low level flat roof abuts cavity wall
When low and high levels are built at the same time, two methods are possible.

1 The cavity continues above and below the cavity cloak, **2**.
If this method is used, the cavity cloak dpc material should be robust and site supervisors must ensure care in cleaning out. Damage to the dpc material may not be noticed and, even if it *is* seen, it will be impossible to repair without taking out brickwork. A metal dpc is probably best, but some very tough bituminous compounds would also be suitable. Laps in the dpc need to be welted, welded or otherwise sealed together, as water would run along and drip through an ordinary lap joint.

2 It may be considered preferable to build the lower wall as solid rather than cavity construction, **3**. This is possibly cheaper and gives slightly more space to the low building. The cavity flashing can then be supported.

Peter Woodcock commented: 'Method **3** is open to criticism for providing a perfect cold bridge.'

Cecil Handisyde replied: 'Although the one-brick walling and concrete corbel unit is in fact no worse than in the original building, the criticism is quite fair.'

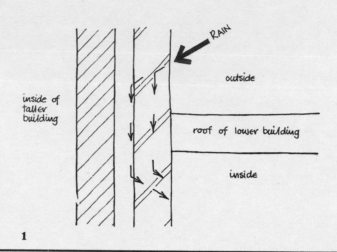

2

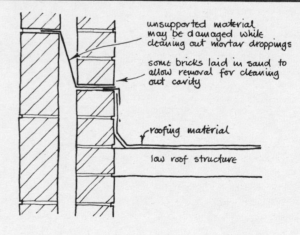

3

Low level pitched roof abuts high cavity wall

The principles are similar to those where the low building is flat roofed, but the detailing of a satisfactory cloak and flashing becomes much more complicated and it is worth considering the alternative of weatherproofing the upper wall with an external treatment.

If the pitched roof is tiled or slated there should be soakers, covered by an apron flashing in short lengths and lapped, **4a**. Alternatively, the apron flashing can be separate from the cavity cloak, **4b**.

The cavity cloak must be stepped at frequent intervals, with each step arranged so that the water from the higher level is discharged on to and *not behind* the next lower level. Each length of cavity cloak should at least oversail the next lower length by about 75 mm, **5**.

In stepped terrace housing pitched roofs, the exposed upper walling is not more than a few hundred mm high, and often protected by a verge overhang. There must be enough working space below this to install the flashing.

James Guest of Belfast commented: 'The flashings detail in both **2** and **4b** is suspect. You indicate the stepped apron flashing coming below the main cavity flashing; if this detail is put into operation water will undoubtedly be drawn by capillary action to the inside of the outer leaf.'

Cecil Handisyde replied: 'It is considered that the methods shown in **2** and **4b** would often be adequate, but I agree that the **4a** method is better and should be preferred on exposed sites.'

Bitter experience taught **R. L. Haynes** and **S. J. Morris** of Beckingsdale & Partners that **5** does not always work. The arrangement illustrated had several weaknesses, they claimed.
'1 Water collected by the stepped cavity tray may discharge water the "wrong" way over the end where there is no stepped cavity cloak beneath, so discharging water down the cavity.
2 There is an area of exposed brickwork below the stepped cavity cloak and above the stepped apron flashing where water may enter.
3 Part of the cavity cloak discharges below the apron flashing preventing water being discharged externally at all. There is a proprietary type of cavity tray and gutter which overcomes these problems. It consists of a preformed metal tray with upstands at the back and one side and is built into the outer skin. A lead apron flashing is fixed to the tray which is dressed over the tiles or into a secret gutter.'

Cecil Handisyde replied:
'1 I agree that there could be the weakness described.
2 There *is* a very small area of exposed brick.
3 I cannot see where the outlet would get significantly blocked.'

Tom Kay wrote: 'In 1965, I experienced a great deal of trouble with exactly the detail you have suggested in **5**. Admittedly I used a semi-engineering brick whose lack of porosity tended to overload the brick joints with water. A part of the wall was finally taken down and rebuilt, using a complex and very expensive lead-formed continuously-stepped cavity tray—much to my embarrassment at the time (see drawing and photograph, next page).
'Assuming well-laid bricks of average, or above, porosity and a relatively soft mortar, your detail might work, but with an overlap between trays of more like 300 mm than the 75 mm

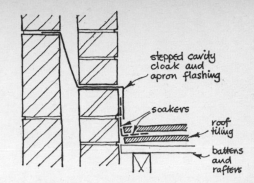

4a

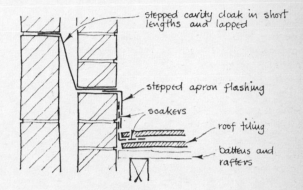

4b

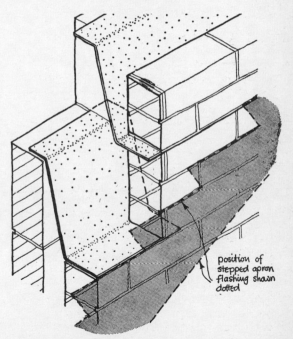

5

stated as desirable in your text. However, if weep holes are positioned anywhere within the cavity wall, the detail will not work at all, because, in windy conditions, a negative pressure is set up within the cavity, which draws the water through any faulty joints (and there always are a few) and pulls it along the cavity tray until it drops off the end and into the building below.
'This latter trouble occurred on another building in 1967, where the laps in the cavity trays were 150 mm and, that time, it was much to my cost. The building was finally soaked in a silicone solution.'

Cecil Handisyde replied: 'This does seem to be rather an expensive solution but it does emphasise that the cost of doing a proper job on this type of detail will always be high.'

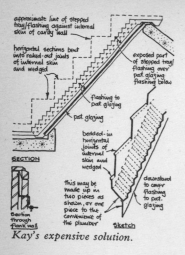

Kay's expensive solution.

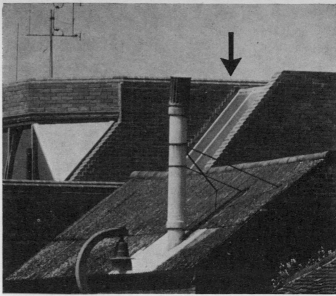

Position of Kay's cavity tray.

New extension to existing higher building

Low level flat roof
The method shown in **2** is possible but would have to be done by removing short lengths of the existing outer wall of the cavity which would be expensive.

Two alternatives might be considered:

1 If visually acceptable, the upper exposed cavity wall could be externally waterproofed, eg by rendering, tile hanging or cladding with timber or other material. The cost would depend on the extent of upper wall there was to be treated.

If a single-storey extension is built next to a building of several storeys, it may be necessary only to protect one storey above the extension. Rain entering above that level would be unlikely to soak through and run down a whole storey. Cavity should be ventilated.

2 The 'wet' leaf of the cavity wall adjacent to the extension might be waterproofed, **6**.

The advisability of the second method is questionable. Severity of exposure of the upper walling should be considered, together with the type of walling material, eg a dense impermeable brick in strong mortar may be more susceptible to water entry through joints than an absorbent brick in a weak mortar.

If method 2 is used, some outlet at the bottom of the wall should be formed as a precaution against build-up of water. Good ventilation to the upper cavity walling would help to dry out water, but if adequate for this purpose it would significantly reduce the thermal insulation value of the cavity and would not permit cavity fill to be used.

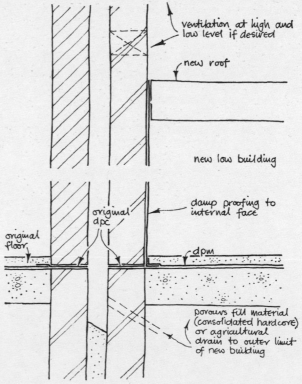

6

Low level pitched roof
The difficulties referred to in adding cavity gutter protection above a flat roof building extension are greater if the complicated system of **5** is to be inserted.

A further solution for both flat and pitched roofs
One solution, if the loss of 150 mm of space is not vital, is to build a completely new leaf, **7** (which might be useful structurally too). It is also a practical solution to the problem of a new pitched roof abutting an existing wall.

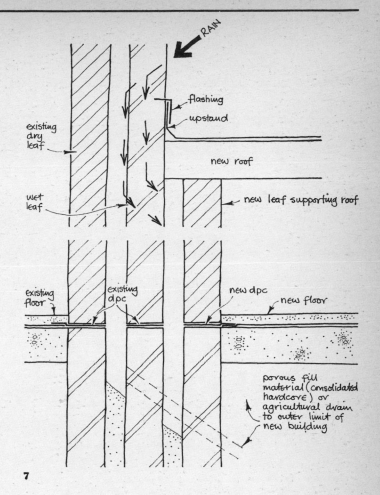

7

17

Wind damage to roofs

Introduction

This detail is unlike any other in this book in that it does not offer direct design and construction guidance.
The Everyday Details team had great difficulty in reaching agreement on the best method of assessing potential wind damage to roofs and on the design implications of wind loading. The team decided, therefore, merely to state the recommendations and procedures contained in the Code of Practice, commenting on the difficulties these raise, and throwing the problem over to readers to help in formulating generalised design guidance.

The size of the problem

Estimates indicate that in the UK the annual cost of repairs to building necessitated by wind damage amounts to £10 million. A large part of this relates to structural roof damage and much occurs as damage to small buildings. If, as is believed, the incidence of damage is increasing, this probably results in part from the gradual introduction of a number of changes in design without a full recognition of their combined effect. Lighter weight structure is one factor and the use of low pitched roofs is another. There are also less obvious changes such as the decreasing use of purlin construction, and the increasing use of single span structures without intermediate support and fixing, eg trussed rafters. A general deterioration in the quality of workmanship may also be significant.

Living with the regulations

The need for positive action to provide adequate safeguards is officially recognised by Building Regulations referring to CP 3 *Basic data for the design of buildings*, Chapter V Loading: Part 2 Wind loads. BRE Digest 119 provides a useful aid to understanding the problem. A more recent and more elaborate publication is *Wind loading handbook* by C. W. Newberry and K. J. Eaton (HMSO). In reviewing this handbook Allan Hodgkinson said of the code 'it is doubtful whether many architects understand it or many engineers believe it but as a statutory document blessed by the Building Regulations it is necessary to live with it'. We suspect that many local authorities do not insist on evidence of calculations for small buildings and that designers often opt out of the onerous calculation process. Meanwhile high repair costs continue and, from time to time, an exceptional gale causes massive damage to property—and to the reputation of architects.

Application of the code

In what follows we are concerned only with the application to roofs of CP 3: Chapter V: Part 2. The code recommendations can be considered in three main stages:
A Assessing design wind speed
B Converting design wind speed to dynamic pressure
C Determining correct pressure for particular parts of a roof.
The design of construction details to provide for safe resistance to the determined conditions is not within the scope of this code.

A Evaluation of wind speed

1 Determine basic wind speed for the geographical location

Values are based on a 3 second gust speed estimated to be exceeded once in 50 years.

Comments: Does this mean that one should design for an average building to receive damage once in its lifetime? (See 4 below.)

As might be expected the wind speeds show a general increase from low in the South east to high in the West and North and very high in the North-west, but it may surprise some people to find equal values for Plymouth and Leicester. Designers working outside their familiar areas need to be careful. It may also be noted that apparently small differences in wind speed assume considerable importance when multiplied by all the factors, eg by interpolation on the contour map Leeds has a wind speed of 47 but in the list of cities a speed of 46. The resultant pressures emerge as 4748 and 4587—a difference of 4·5 per cent.

2 Adjust basic wind speed for topography (S_1 factor)

Basic wind speed is adjusted by a factor, normally between 1·1 and 0·9. The high value applies to exposed hill slopes and crests and to valleys shaped to produce wind funnelling. The low factor is used for valleys sheltered to all winds.

Comments: The code makes no direct reference here to coastal situations but covers itself with a reference to the value of local knowledge and to the possible need to obtain further advice from the meteorological office (see also 3 below).

3 Adjust for local conditions (S_2 factor)

The conditions considered are ground roughness and the size and height of the subject building. For each combination of local ground condition and height above ground of a part of the building three factor values are given. These three values depend upon assumptions about wind gust duration. The highest factor values (for 3 second gust enveloping unit of 20 m horizontal or vertical dimension) apply primarily to glazing, cladding and roof finishes and their immediate fixings. Intermediate values (for 5 second gust enveloping a 50 m unit) apply to building structures of small to moderately large size, while lowest values (for 15 second gust on buildings over 50 m height or width) apply to large structures. The conversion factors range from 0·47 to 1·27 or, if the high values applicable only to 'cladding' are omitted, the range becomes 0·47 to 1·24.

Comments: This local factor has a considerably wider range of influence than the S_1 topography factor. The code does here refer to sites on cliffs or escarpments and an appendix provides a guide to calculation for those situations.

Table I Comparative wind speeds and pressures for two contrasting areas in the UK

Basic wind speed V (metres/second)		Greater London area 38 m/s Worst case	Best case	East Pennines 46 m/s Worst case	Best case
S_1 factor	Exposed Sheltered	1·1 —	— 0·9	1·1 —	— 0·9
S_2 factor	Worst ground approach and building shape combination Best combination	1·24 —	— 0·47	1·24 —	— 0·47
S_3 factor	100 year life 50 year life	1·22 —	— 1·0	1·22 —	— 1·0
Design wind speed $V_S = V \times S_1 \times S_2 \times S_3$ m/s		$38 \times 1·1 \times 1·24 \times 1·22$ = 63·2 m/s	$38 \times 0·9 \times 0·47 \times 1·0$ = 16·0 m/s	$46 \times 1·1 \times 1·24 \times 1·22$ = 76·5 m/s	$46 \times 0·9 \times 0·47 \times 1·0$ = 19·5 m/s
Equivalent basic pressure $q = 0·613 \, V^2$ N/m²		2448 N/m²	157 N/m²	3587 N/m²	233 N/m²

4 Possibly adjust for building life and acceptable risk (S_3 factor)

This is a statistical exercise. The designer has to decide from the type of building and its probable life what degree of risk to accept. The code suggests some cases which may need consideration but broadly indicates that a value of $S_3 = 1$ is appropriate representing a probability of 0·636 in a 50 year life, ie there is a 1 in 1·6 chance of the design wind speed being exceeded at least once in 50 years but without any assessment of the excess, ie the safety factor may or may not prevent a failure.

Comment: Will the increasing tendency for clients to sue architects on this issue be defensible on the grounds of reasonable professional judgment, or should a designer refer the matter to his client—who probably would not be able to judge the situation? (See also comment in 1 above.)

5 Determine design wind speed (V_S)

Design wind speed = basic wind speed (V) $\times S_1 \times S_2 \times S_3$

Comment: Examples given in table I may be somewhat unrealistic in combining 'all worst' possibilities and comparing to 'all best', but chosen in that way they do emphasise the importance of decisions made during this stage of the assessment. Table I shows the build up from basic wind speed to design wind speed for two cases in the Greater London region and two similar cases in the proximity of Leeds. In the S_2 factors the high values that would relate only to roof finishes and their immediate fixings have not been applied in these examples.

B Dynamic wind pressure (q)

The code gives a formula, $q = kV^2$, for converting design wind speed into dynamic pressure of wind where k is a factor depending on the type of units used eg, for S_1 units N/m² and m/s, the k value is 0·613. Table II is a reproduction of the code table 4.

Table II Values of q in SI units (N/m²) (Taken from CP 3: Chapter V; Part 2, table 4)

V_S m/s	0	1·0	2·0	3·0	4·0	5·0	6·0	7·0	8·0	9·0
10	61	74	88	104	120	138	157	177	199	221
20	245	270	297	324	353	383	414	447	481	516
30	552	589	628	668	709	751	794	839	885	932
40	981	1030	1080	1130	1190	1240	1300	1350	1410	1470
50	1530	1590	1660	1720	1790	1850	1920	1990	2060	2130
60	2210	2280	2360	2430	2510	2590	2670	2750	2830	2920
70	3000									

C Assessment of wind loads on parts of buildings

The dynamic pressure (q) has to be multiplied by a coefficient that depends upon the shape and size of the building. The code employs two types of coefficient:
1 pressure coefficient (cp)
2 force coefficient (cf)
The pressure coefficients apply to the particular surface of a building and can be combined to give the total pressure acting on the building as a whole. To avoid this calculation the code assesses this directly and expresses it as a force coefficient.

Table 8 of the code gives pressure coefficient values (Cpe) for pitched roofs of rectangular buildings.

Comments: Since the table covers pitches from 0 to 60 degrees it in fact deals with flat roofs in spite of its heading. A separate table covers monopitch roofs.

The term Cpe indicates external pressure. It appears however that the effect of wind entering through open doorways, windows etc can have a significant effect, eg by adding an upward pressure to the underside of a roof. A description of how to assess this is provided in an appendix to the code. In some cases the additional pressure may need calculation but for the peace of mind of architects it may be noted that where there is only a negligible probability of a dominant opening occurring during a severe storm the coefficient for internal wind (Cpi) should be taken as the more onerous of $+ 0·2$ and $-0·3$.

The data in table 8 of the code divides buildings into three groups according to height/width ratio. For each group it gives pressure coefficients for wind directions towards the long side or short side of the buildings. These values refer to the main areas of a roof. Additional, higher value coefficients are given for local areas ie eaves, verges and ridges.
Since on most sites it must be assumed that wind may blow from any direction a composite picture must be formed, allocating to each roof area the worst Cpe that could apply.

Complications: It must not be assumed that a satisfactory assessment has now been achieved: uplift due to eaves projection will need to be allowed for. Parapets and other roof projections can raise further complications. The code states that pressure on roof overhangs is to be taken as the same as that on the adjoining wall surface. (Other tables and diagrams in the code are used for assessing this.) The protective effect of parapets is not referred to in the code but is dealt with in the handbook. If the effects of eaves or other complications are ignored it is clear from the code values that uplift around roof perimeters is greatest with flat roofs, with a Cpe coefficient of −2·0 for all shapes of building. For pitched roofs perimeter values vary both with angle of roof pitch and with the height/width ratio of the building.

If the code Cpe values are applied to the 'best' or 'worst' East Pennines area situations from table I with an assumption that the roofs are flat and without complications of eaves, parapets etc, the external pressure coefficients, taking account of all wind directions, would be as in **1**.

Final estimations of wind uplift values can now be made and are shown in table III. Although the two examples are extreme cases, and not strictly comparable, they illustrate the very wide range of conditions that appear to be possible in one area of the country.

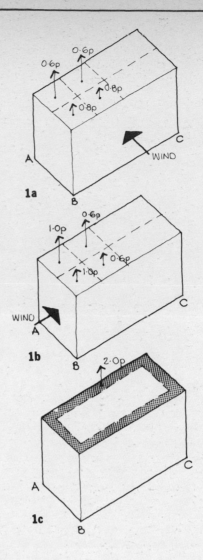

Table III Estimation of wind uplift for wind condition shown in 1

| Condition | Basic wind speed 46 m/s | |
	Worst case (N/m²)	Best case (N/m²)
Uplift on centre area	3587 × 1·0 = 3587	233 × 1·0 = 233
Uplift on end area	3587 × 1·2 = 4304	233 × 1·2 = 280
Uplift due to local effects (for cladding and fixings)	3587 × 2·2 = 7891	233 × 2·2 = 513

D The implications of the calculations

Whether or not calculations based on the code provide an accurate assessment of site conditions is questioned by some engineers but, even if the results are only very approximate, they indicate the importance of an aspect of building safety that until recently has been almost ignored in most books on building construction and which even in recent works has generally received only slight attention.

There seem to be three main constructional problems to consider:

Security of outer roof coverings
Existing codes of practice (eg CP 142 *Slating and tiling* or CP 143 *Sheet roof and wall coverings*) deal with securing external finishes. If their recommendations are sound then with the exception of very severe exposure conditions the fixing for outer finishes can follow these codes and the wind load CP 3 need not be applied. One wonders, however, how finishes such as loosely bonded sheet material, or asphalt on a loose underlay, could withstand the suction values that result from code calculations.

Preventing damage to main roof structure
For many types of structure this may mean examining the following categories of fixings:

1 Decking: eg boards, sheets or slabs, sited immediately beneath roof finishes. The fixing of these units to supporting members such as rafters, beams or walls.

2 The fixing of intermediate supports, eg rafters or small beams to larger more widely spaced members.

3 The fixing of final roof support members to walls. Designers may find two types of problem at this stage:

1 *Wind pressures on a building in the East Pennines, assuming a basic wind speed of 46 m/s. In the worst case, equivalent basic pressure q = 3587 N/m², and in the best case q = 233 N/m² (see table I).*
a, b *Wind is blowing at 90° to the building face and pressure values are shown for the centre area. If there is a dominant opening facing the wind the values are increased. If no specific calculation is made, normal permeability should be allowed for by adding 0·2p to the pressure values shown.*
c *Wind is blowing at an angle to the building face other than 90° and the pressure value for the end area is shown. Depending on the angle, pressures of 2p can develop locally but not everywhere at one time. Again these values are increased as in a and b for permeability. Calculations are shown in table III.*

(a) To determine how load transfer occurs through a roof structure and therefore what load conditions need to be met for positions 2 or 3 above.

(b) To determine a realistic value for various types of fixing. Steel bolted to steel can be reasonably assessed but what is the value of a nail? How can a laboratory test result be translated to the probable value of a haphazardly driven nail put in by a disgruntled workman operating on a cold and windy site? What is the achieved value for the not altogether unusual 'fixing' of a wallplate which according to some construction books is 'bedded in mortar'?

The effect of roof uplift on wall stability

This discussion has been directed to wind damage to roofs but the code is also a guide to design for walls. Lateral stability of walls is often dependent upon roof support. If wind lifts the roof then support to walls may be lost. The location and detailed design of roof to wall fixings must take this aspect into account. To what extent must roof to wall anchorage do more than just overcome the roof uplift force?

Comments: Two letters sent in response to detail 17 as originally published in *The Architects' Journal* are printed below. Correspondence was also received from the Marley Tile Company, drawing attention to advice they have prepared in the form of a roofing specification. This tabulates fixing for tiles by clipping and by nailing, taking into account building height, site exposure and wind speed.

From **Bernard Warren:** 'With reference to wind damage to roofs, the experience of this corporation may be of some interest to you. You may recall that in February 1962 there was a considerable amount of damage by wind in this city [Sheffield] and the city architect's department at that time produced a report on the damage which occurred, together with recommendations for future construction which endeavoured to reduce the risk of some other damage in future. This report was published in *The Builder* on 5 October 1962.

While there were many and varied types of damage to new buildings, the general impression was that the most difficulty occurred when there had been reductions in the standards of specifications in an endeavour to reduce the cost of building, which were then added to by a reduction in the quality and standard of workmanship on the site. The combination of these two factors appeared almost certain to cause failure to a greater or lesser extent. Following this report the specifications for roof constructions and detailing generally used in this city by the city council were considerably improved on what had previously been standard.

The numerical majority of failures was clearly in tiled and slated roofs and, in an endeavour to reduce such failures in all corporation work incorporating such roofs, it has since 1962 been specified that each tile or slate must be nailed or clipped to the roof. The ridge tiles should be fully bedded in cement, and preferably with a mechanical fix to the roof structure by means of wire ties or other suitable systems It must be appreciated that this is what is specified but it is known that the workmen on site, usually on bonus, do not always provide the 100 per cent fixing specified but a reduction of even 50 per cent in what was required is far better than a reduction of 50 per cent on a specification which calls for every third or even fifth course of tiles to be nailed.'

D. Evans Palmer wrote: 'The only wind damage to the buildings designed by this practice in seventy-five years occurred about 1956, when a narrow belt of high wind, which took out trees, lifted a bus shelter and a stadium roof, also lifted an asbestos cement sheeted roof complete with rafters off a row of a dozen garages and laid it upside down on the ground. The purlins pulled out of the stone wall, breaking the bed joints in the process and the upward force was later calculated to be of the order of 80 lbs per sq ft.

'The client's insurers paid, without question, for direct and consequential damage. This was an exceptional gale; it caused massive damage to property but not—and this is the point—*not* to the reputation of any architects. And why should it?

'The threat to reputation arises at two levels: call them judgment and competence, judgment bearing on *what* we do and competence on *how* we do it. The "Comment" at 4 (page 77) sums the problem up but until we sort it out it is not easy to know the basis on which further information on this, and similar subjects, should be published.

'Easier for the architect and more profitable to (over) design for any and every risk, even catastrophe. More difficult and more expensive to work to the hazy limits of CP 3 and the design of the construction details themselves to follow.

'My contention is that the reasonable exercise of professional judgment should afford a defence against an action for negligence in all but exceptional circumstances, while a failure of competence, in the implementation of that judgment, should be fair game.

'There is a distinction between the two which, though difficult to describe is, like the elephant, easy to recognise.'

18

Flat roofs: falls

For many years codes of practice and most specialist roofing contractors have called for slight falls in 'flat' roofs, usually 1:80 for well laid smooth finishes such as asphalt and 1:60 for sheet coverings with sealed laps. Because of cost or problems of detailing, or the effect upon appearance of verges, designers have not always provided such falls. In other cases the slight falls provided for in design have not been achieved in practice, either because of inaccuracies in construction or because of deflection after completion.

Are falls necessary?

Where roofs are overlooked from above, falls may be considered necessary in order to avoid unsightly puddles. Falls may be thought advisable as a precaution against *serious* flooding if a leak occurs.

A common reason put forward for the need for falls has been the probable increase in the rate of deterioration of roof membranes when exposed to alternate wetting and drying around puddles.

BRE Digest 144 (August 1972)* gave damning evidence of the general inefficiency of flat roof finishes but did not give a clear lead on whether falls are necessary. The digest said that ponding is less harmful to the roof covering than was at one time supposed. It is not clear whether 'less harmful' means it can be accepted. Later in the digest ponding is referred to as causing crazing on asphalt finishes 'which may be only shallow' and in the condition shown on one illustration 'does not warrant the cost of remedial treatment unless on grounds of appearance'.

Certain felts are held to have greater resistance to wet/dry deterioration than others. Rag based felts should never be laid without effective falls.

Falls should be omitted only after very careful consideration of particular situations, including roof size, frequency of outlets, basic roof structure, and type of waterproofing finish, and only in agreement with the roofing contractor. Because falls materially affect design appearance, detailing and cost, a basic decision must be made early—often before consultation with the roofing specialist who will eventually carry out the work is feasible. Hence, the responsibility for effective roof performance must lie with the architect.

Minimum falls

It is suggested that minimum falls should be 1:80 for smooth surfaces and 1:60 otherwise. These are to be *achieved* falls after allowing for building inaccuracy, main structure and roof deck deflection or creep (all of which are difficult to estimate so allowances must be generous). Note, for example, that on floor screeds a tolerance of ±3 mm over 3 m, and ±10 mm across large areas is a normal specification allowance.

Care in detailing is needed to avoid checks to the flow of water, **1ab**, **2ab**.

This is a problem which occurs not only at the eaves. It can happen on joints running across the fall, **2a**. If the lap causes a 3 mm upstand at a slope of 1:60 the ponding could extend 60 × 3 = 1·8 m back from the lap.

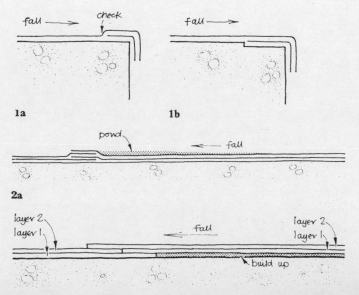

* Published by the Building Research Establishment

The answer to avoiding ponding probably lies in careful workmanship gradually to build up the bottom layer over the last few metres to make up for the thickness of the lower sheet, **2b**. Otherwise the pitch of the roof must be increased.

Roof fall arrangements

The feasibility of a roof fall arrangement is often related to roof construction. Internal rwps must be related to internal planning and all rwp positioning affects underground drains. It is essential therefore to determine roof arrangements at an early design stage.

The following diagrams show various arrangements of roof falls and water disposal with notes on some of the advantages and disadvantages of each type.

One-way fall to external gutter

The basic arrangement is shown in **3**. Ways of achieving it are described below.

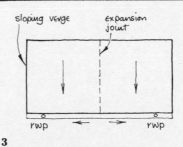

3

Structure

Shaped beams or joists, flat ceiling, **4a**.

4a

Flat beams or joists, simple firring, flat ceiling, **4b**.

4b

Sloping beams or joists, sloping or flat suspended ceiling, **4c**.

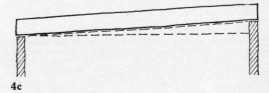

4c

Sloping slab, sloping ceiling, **4d**.

4d

Flat slab screeded, **4e**.
This may result in very thick screed. Heavier and more expensive than **4d**.

4e

Sheet decking on firring to falls on a flat slab, **4f**. Common on the continent. One system available here uses wood wool on precast concrete firrings. The void space provides some chance of ventilation to the external air to prevent water vapour pressure and condensation.

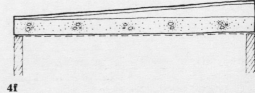

4f

Sloping slab, suspended ceiling, **4g**.
Structurally the one-way fall is most likely to suit short or medium span buildings. On long buildings a roof expansion joint can run in direction of falls.

Gutters and rwps

Minimum number and cost. Blockage immediately obvious.

4g

Drains

Minimum number. None beneath building.

Appearance

Visible gutter and rwps (unless behind a parapet). End verges slope unless detailed with a parapet or upstand. If end verges are detailed with parapet or upstand, the corner junction with the external gutter may be unacceptable in appearance.

Two-way falls to external gutters

The basic arrangement is shown in **5a**. Ways of achieving it are described below.

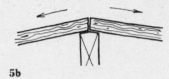

Structure

Normally used for wider spans than **3**. For similar spans, there is less build-up of screeds or firring than **3**. For unshaped joists or beams, laying to fall is only possible if two members meet over an intermediate support, **5b**. Expansion joints can run with falls.

5a   **5b**

Gutters and rwps

Gutters are double the length of roof **3**. Rwps probably more than roof **3**.

Drains

From two sides of building. Expensive if to main drain disposal but less important with soakaway system.

Appearance

Roof **3** factors apply, but end verge slopes are two-way balanced.

Four-way falls to external gutters

The basic arrangement is shown in **6**.

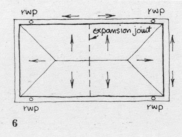

Structure

Except for screeded roofs, the cross falls introduce complications but tapered timber or lattice steel girders can be fixed to form hips.

6

Gutter and rwps and drains

Rwps and drains may be similar to roof type **5**. Gutter length is increased. The tendency is to limit gutter falls to absolute minimum and extreme care is needed to maintain line and avoid backfalls.

Appearance

Gutter is similar all round. Obviates sloping verges of types **3** and **5**.

Four-way falls to single internal outlet

The basic arrangement is shown in **7**.

Structure
Except for screeded roofs the cross falls introduce difficulties. Any required expansion joint is difficult to locate satisfactorily.

Rwps
Must be located to suit internal plan. Single outlet may become blocked and remain unnoticed. Large build-up of water weight may occur. A very wide bore rwp (say 200 mm) with protective basket should be trouble free. (This policy is usually adopted in large industrial buildings even if the rwp connects to a 150 mm drain.)

Drains
Economical single point drain, but early installation requirement involves accurate positioning for later connection to rwp.

Appearance
All verges similar.

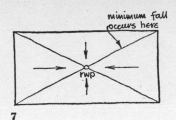

7

Four-way falls to multiple internal outlets

The basic arrangement is shown in **8**.

Structure
Generally similar to type **7** but location of expansion joint is easier.

Rwps
The introduction of multiple rwps does not substantially reduce risk of water build-up from blockage because outlets are separated by a high ridge line (large outlets again advisable).

Drains
More drainage needed than for type **7**.

Appearance
All verges similar.

8

Four-way falls to two outlets and valley

The basic arrangement is shown in **9**.
Generally similar to **8** but at the risk of some pooling of water along the valley. The outlets can act as alternatives if one is blocked.
Expansion joint can be reasonably located.

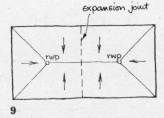

9

Roof falling to internal gutters

The basic arrangement is shown in **10a**.

Structure
Simple roof falls, but structure must be able to accommodate gutter depth including falls. This may be difficult if roof structure is basically at right angles to gutter. Expansion joint continuity across gutter raises problems. Risk of single rwp blockage. Some relief may be obtained by weir overflows at external ends of gutter.
Two rwps, **10b**, are better than **10a** for blockage of outlets but there is extra cost for rwp and drains.
Location of expansion joint does not cause problems.
Both **10a** and **b** are acceptable if there is structural support along and under the internal gutter.

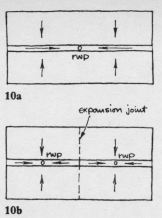

10a

10b

Internal drainage generally

Unless a flat roof is easily visible from higher buildings in the same occupancy, blockage of outlets may remain unnoticed. Clients should be advised on the need for regular checks. The probability of adequate inspection will be affected by ease of access to the roof.
Snow and ice are frequent cause of temporary blockage. Grids over internal gutters can help but protection of outlets in roof types **8** to **10** is difficult.
Unless *regular* maintenance can be expected it is questionable whether internal gutters or outlets should be used on low buildings with trees nearby, **11**.
In addition to acceptable location of gutters and rwps to suit internal plan arrangement, the possibility of noise nuisance from internal pipes should be considered. Bends increase the risk of noise.
Internal gutters should not be allowed to reduce thermal insulation and thus form cold bridges with a consequential risk of condensation. Condensation may also occur on surfaces of rwps chilled by cold rainwater, in heated buildings.
Leakage from internal rwps can be disastrous. Joints must be adequate. Consider possible build-up of pressure if low level blockage occurs and how trouble can be cured without flooding the building in the process.

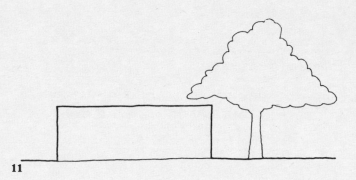

11

19

Flat roofs: timber joist construction

Detail 18 considered in general terms the need for falls on 'flat' roofs and how the arrangement of falls affects efficiency and appearance. In this detail the provision of falls to roofs of timber construction is considered in more detail.

There are three basic methods:

1 to provide a sloping roof deck by forming falls in the below-deck structure, **1**;

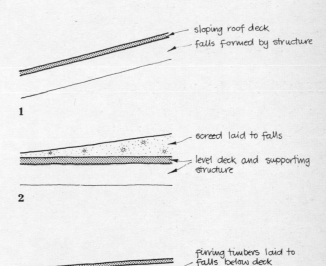

2 to form a level deck and above that to lay screed or shaped insulation material to provide falls, **2**;

3 to form a level structure by using unshaped joists and forming falls by firring timbers below the deck, **3**.

In the second and third methods the basic roof construction can be designed virtually without regard to roof falls except where internal gutters are required which must be able to run parallel to and within the depth of roof members.

Until recently, roof falls formed above deck level were generally restricted to screeded roofs, **2** (a system more suitable for concrete deck systems). Lately lightweight wedge shaped roof insulating slabs have been used. It is worth noting that to meet a need for much higher standards of thermal insulation, and as a precaution against interstitial condensation on the underside of impermeable roof finishes, there may well be an increase in methods using thick insulation on top of a vapour barrier laid on the roof deck, **4**. This may provide an attractive method for forming roof falls although it will be important to resist a temptation to reduce insulation too much at the 'low' ends of falls. It is also of the greatest importance to ensure that whatever light preformed insulation is used it has a surface of sufficient density to stand up to people walking on the roof finish (even if only for maintenance). Considerable problems have been experienced in the use of lightweight polystyrene screeds because of indentation of the roof surface by foot traffic. A higher density polystyrene or polyurethane can avoid this problem.

The remainder of this detail relates to the forming of roof falls beneath the roof deck.

Methods of forming falls below the roof deck

1 Firring parallel with, and on top of, joists.

2 Cross firring (battens of differing thickness—or tapered, depending on the direction of fall) above joists.

3 Joists cut to falls.
(All the above provide level ceilings.)

4 Joists laid to falls. (Resulting in sloping ceilings.)

5 Joists laid to falls plus suspended cross battens or other means to obtain level ceilings.

An important factor in determining choice of the above will be whether the proposed roof falls are parallel to or across the proposed joist direction.

Falls parallel to joist direction

With all variations of this method internal gutters are difficult or impossible to form, unless there is an intermediate structural support (wall or beam).

Because the upper surface of a roof deck should provide and maintain a smooth fall, decking of square edged timber boarding laid at right angles across the joists is unsuitable.

Joists laid to falls
Simple and economical, **5**. Sloping ceiling may be unacceptable. A slope exceeding the necessary minimum may look better than a very slight one, and a two-way slope may look better than a monopitch. But this requires a central support in the form of a beam and not a wall as in **7**, where the slopes are visually separated.

Slope is especially noticeable above nearby window heads, **6**. Curtain tracks simply set in ceiling will not work.

Two-way roof falls are feasible only if an internal bearing wall or beam occurs conveniently, **7**. This method does not provide convenience for services or help roof space ventilation inherent in methods using cross firring or suspended ceilings. Roof ventilation might be provided at the ridge through the roof covering.

Joist cut to falls
Example **8** is simple to fix but joists may be more costly than **5** and **7**, but not necessarily since two joists can probably be cut from one scantling. Level ceiling is also an advantage.

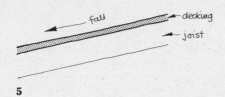

5

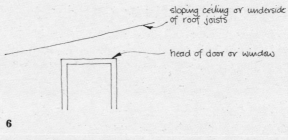

6

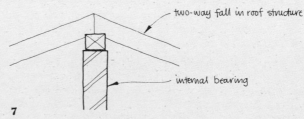

7

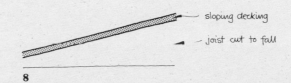

8

Shaping to two-way falls is feasible, **9**. Restriction to services and cross ventilation. When used at fairly wide spacing to support strong decking material, or decking on secondary supports, fabricated beams for main members can be constructed to falls. The cutting of solid joists to falls is unlikely to be feasible because of the sizes of timber required.

Method **10b** allows roof boards to run with the falls. It also provides the advantages over **10a** of cross ventilation and easy service runs.

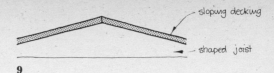

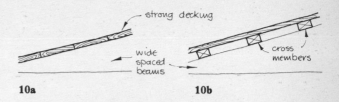

Sloping joists and suspended ceiling

Many proprietary systems are available but site-made constructions with timber battens will almost certainly be more economical for small jobs, **11**. Cross members' sizes depend upon joist spacing. Where roof falls are considerable, this type of construction may use less timber than normal firring above the joists but involve more site labour than those shown previously. Good for cross ventilation. Very convenient for services. If main joists vary slightly in depth this method should overcome the tiresome problem of uneven ceiling levels.

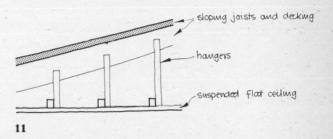

Firring on top of joists

The simplest and usually the most economical method is shown in **12**. All firring pieces are similar. If not obscured by a ceiling the joints between joists and firrings may be unsightly, and increased depth of fascia can be a problem. Does not provide two-way ventilation or easy runs for services. But boring holes or grooving near the end of the spans is simple and does not affect strength. Alternatively, if at centre span, the holes may be drilled through the firring or at mid-depth of the joist.

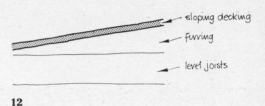

Falls at right angles to joist direction

With this arrangement internal gutters can usually be located between joists, **13**. Note that the gutter also needs falls, the extent of which are limited by the joist depth (d). Insulation will be required under the gutter.

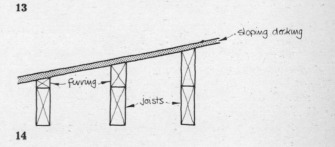

Firring on top of and parallel to joists

14 uses less timber than **15** but each firring piece differs in depth so labour is expensive. Any unequal spacing of joists, a not infrequent condition, means pre-cut firring would be incorrect in depth. Does not provide cross ventilation or easy service runs. This system really has only one advantage: the firring can be reduced to zero at the lowest point; but it is so prone to problems and site difficulties that it is best avoided.

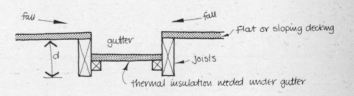

Firring at right angles to joists
15 uses more timber than **14**, as firring cannot be *less than*
50 mm at low point. This means a thicker roof and slight
increase in perimeter 'wall' height. Less labour than **14**.
Provides cross ventilation and space for easy service runs.

**Joists set on shaped wall plates or wall plates fixed to
a fall**
Although **16** is seldom used it may suit some situations.
Two-way slopes are feasible. Disadvantage of sloping
ceiling. Does not provide cross ventilation or space for easy
service runs.

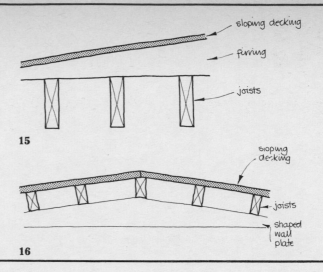

15

16

Choice of roof construction

The examples above illustrate only basic factors.
Complications may arise as in **17**. Internal walls may lead to
variation in joist depth for economy (eg in areas A and B)
or to changes in joist direction (eg in area C).

This may involve changing the method of obtaining falls
or could influence the basic choice of roof fall arrangement,
with consequential change to gutters, rwps and drains.

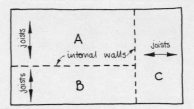

17

In **18**, the introduction of projecting roof area C may
complicate an otherwise simple two-way roof. Firring over
C, continued up roof area B, means increased thickness for
all firring over total roof area B and possibly, therefore, over
roof A. There may also be visual or structural detailing
problems as a result of variation in levels along verges
x, y and z.

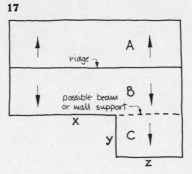

18

What possible solutions are there?

1 Accept the extra cost of deeper firring.

2 Use sloping joists and accept sloping ceiling.

3 Use sloping joists and provide suspended ceiling.

4 Treat roof areas A and B normally and provide beam
between B and C (if no internal wall). In any case, if no
support is provided at that point the joists spanning
section B/C would have to be structurally deeper than the
rest which would, in itself, create a problem whatever
system of providing falls were adopted.

20

Flat roofs: verges of timber joist roofs

Criteria

It is not feasible to illustrate all the possible roof verge variations but any proposed design should be checked against the following criteria:

1 adequacy of fixing of roof to walls or structure to prevent damage to the roof from wind suction, **1**;

2 adequacy of fixing of roof to walls or structure to ensure any necessary lateral support to prevent damage to walls from wind, **2**;

3 the need to provide slight or considerable ventilation of roof voids either to prevent deterioration of vulnerable materials or, where materials are resistant, to prevent build-up of interstitial condensation, **3**;

4 the need to ensure that all materials at the verge are suitable for their situation, **4**;

5 the need to ensure that water from the verge, including wind-blown overspill from the roof, will not damage or disfigure the walling, **5**;

6 the need to avoid cold bridging caused by lack of continuity of thermal insulation, **6**;

7 the possible need to provide for thermal movement of edge trim and to ensure that provision for movement does not permit water entry, **7**;

8 whether the detailing is reasonable in allowing a satisfactory sequence of building operations, in particular whether delay in fixing the waterproofing finish would cause trouble, **8**;

9 the need to ensure that all the visual implications of the proposed design have been considered (especially at points through which no section has been detailed), **9**;

10 the need to ensure that all parts of the construction are sufficiently described:
a to facilitate proper estimates of cost,
b to ensure that all materials or components can be available when needed,
c to prevent unnecessary site queries or unsatisfactory ad hoc 'solutions'.

F. H. Skinner wrote: 'The detail shown for the fascia, particularly in reference to item 5 is, I believe, a poor detail. 'I believe that it is much preferable to have the fascia board fixed so that the back of the fascia is on a bearer giving about a 1in projection from the face of the brickwork to the back of the fascia. The detail that you show is bad in the sense that the fascia cannot be truly fixed because there are inaccuracies in the face of the brickwork and the fascia cannot be painted properly. Apart from the aesthetics this is a structural detail which I believe is incorrect.
'I should be interested to have your comments on this, since

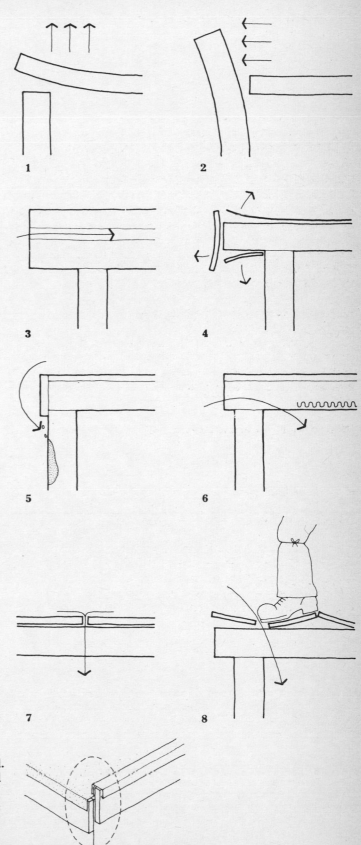

I think it is a small but important detail in respect of both an aesthetic appearance and a good construction.'

The editors replied: 'While agreeing that this alternative has some of the advantages mentioned, the original detail is often used and fixed without apparent difficulty. Re-painting of the vulnerable bottom edge of the fascia would certainly be easier with the batten fixed method.'

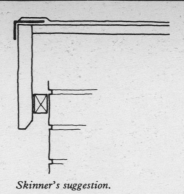

Skinner's suggestion.

The following notes and diagrams deal with some of the matters which arise. To avoid confusion each diagram deals only with limited aspects and therefore is not in itself a full working detail. Further aspects will be covered on pages 94 to 98 and in detail 21.

Details where roof joists are at right angles to wall

A detail similar to **10** is not uncommon but it has several drawbacks, as shown below.

10

The introduction of a wall plate, **11**, should enable better fixing of joists than **10** (providing the wall plate itself is adequately fixed down). The wall plate should ensure good levelling of joists to receive ceiling. With **10** method levels may vary. If wall finish is plaster, the wall plate adds to movement problems and reinforcement is necessary. Although better than **10**, fixing may still be insufficient if wall plate is secured only by bedding in mortar.

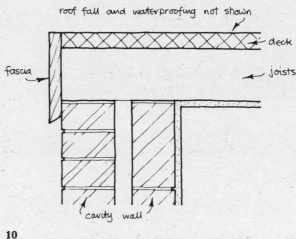

11

On exposed sites where wind uplift is considerable, holding-down straps may be needed, **12**. The length and frequency of strap fixings will depend upon wind load assumptions (see detail 17, page 76).

With this arrangement the value of a wall plate would be to ensure joist levels. An alternative method is to 'strap' down the wall plate and fix joists to it.

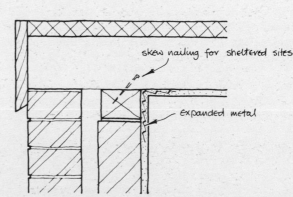
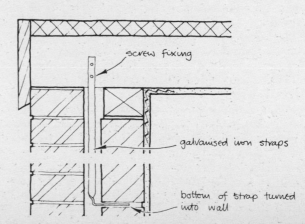

12

With the wall cavity open to the roof voids cavity moisture can be transferred. This adds to the risk of condensation and possible damage, **13**.

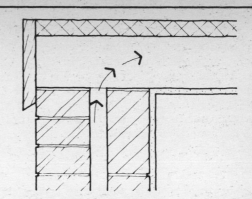

13

Closing the cavity below joist level with solid material for full width of the wall results in a possible path for rain penetration, **14**. The wall might be protected by an increased depth of fascia. The solid closure reduces wall insulation and increases risk of internal surface condensation where trouble is most common. (This would be more likely if all walling was of dense material.)

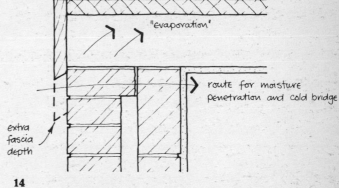

14

Beam filling could form a partial barrier between wall cavity and roof spaces, **15**. It is unlikely to be very effective as tight jointing between joists and beam fills is unobtainable. Beam filling would inhibit cross ventilation.

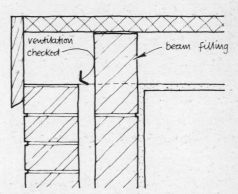

15

A vapour-proof membrane, stuck with adhesive, would form an effective seal to the cavity, **16**. Roof ventilation can be obtained as required. Thermal insulation of walling is maintained. Longitudinal joints in the membrane should be lapped and sealed. Holding down straps (as in **12**) would pierce the membrane, but this would be acceptable (as the extent of the gaps would be so small) if some roof ventilation is provided.

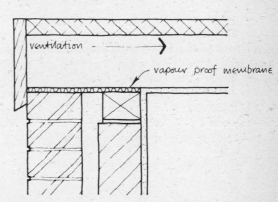

16

Notes on illustrations 10 to 16
Examples **10** to **16** are all of the 'warm roof' system where roof insulation is above the roof deck and is therefore unaffected by the alternatives illustrated. Where the system incorporates thermal insulation at ceiling level care is needed to ensure that its effectiveness is not interrupted by verge detailing.

The structural value of linking the two leaves of a cavity wall by a solid topping has not been mentioned. It is questionable whether a single course brick link adds anything significant to lateral stability. Wall ties (rigid not wire) located near the top of the wall are likely to be more effective. A top course spanning the cavity may be necessary to spread roof loads. This would depend upon the ability of the chosen walling material to carry the loading for a particular situation. Building Regulations require that in some conditions the roof load shall be carried partly by the outer leaf. Even if the cavity is not closed, the load will be shared by both leaves if the joists carry through past the outer bay and are properly seated. See Schedule 7, Clause 11 (6) e.

Details where roof joists are at right angles to wall and project to form a roof overhang

The introduction of the overhang, **17**, exposes the roof to more wind force, so better fixing will be necessary (as in **12**).

The overhang provides some protection to the upper wall and, except on very exposed sites, probably obviates the risk of rain penetration through solid bridging immediately below the roof. Closing the cavity in the way shown would result in a line of exposed headers just under the eaves. This change in bond appearance should be considered.

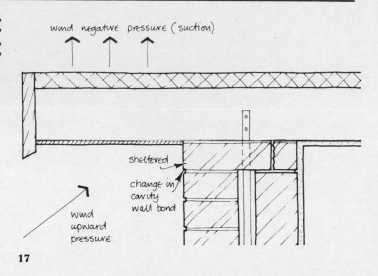

17

Details where roof joists run parallel to wall

A brick or block can close the cavity and support an edge batten. The closure member is not exposed to rain, so a nailable material may be used to facilitate fixing of the timber batten and fascia.

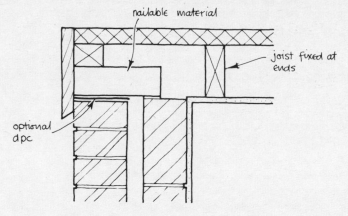

18

If roof joists are adequately secured at their ends and the verge roofing does not project, detail **18** should provide safe fixing for the roof edge on all but very exposed sites.

The arrangement in **18** provides negligible lateral support to the wall. Where this is needed, metal straps should be secured to the wall and turned across the roof joists, **19**. Note the need to allow for wall finish to accommodate the straps. On the ceiling the straps could be recessed into the joists, provided the required minimum joist depth at mid-span is obtained.

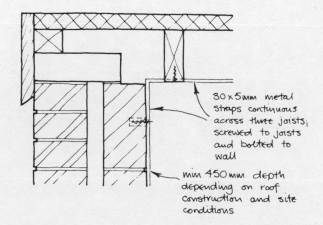

19

Whenever possible it is better to provide any required roof ventilation in the direction of the roof joists. If this is not possible, cross battening is necessary for good ventilation, **20**; this also has the advantage of providing for falls at right angles to joists when required.

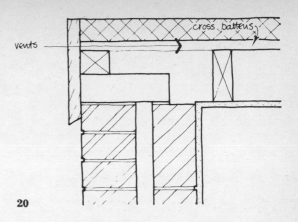

20

Small holes bored at mid-depth of roof joists are sometimes used for ventilation, **21**. Where roof materials are not vulnerable to damage by dampness and conditions require only minor ventilation this method may be adequate. It should not be regarded as suitable where the situation requires a fully ventilated roof.

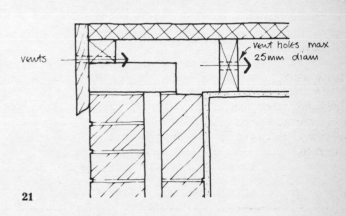

21

Details where joists are parallel to walls and a roof overhang is required

Unless an edge joist (joist 'A'), **22**, spans to suitable fixings, eg projecting walls or secure porch posts, safe fixing, at least on all but very sheltered sites, is questionable with this arrangement.

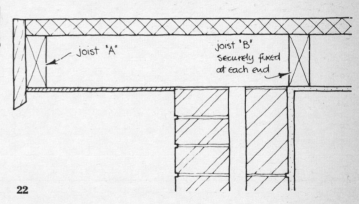

22

Anchorage could be obtained by external ties from the wall to the underside of joist A or some form of strap fixing along the joists and down the cavity might be devised. Where roof construction makes an alteration of the joist direction feasible, it would be better to use the method shown in **23**. For a substantial overhang, the strap fixing should be anchored well down the walling.

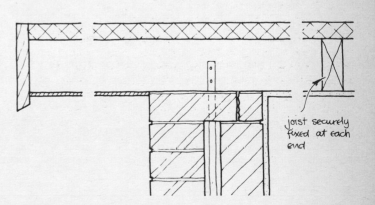

23

Water overflow

It is generally recognised that in the absence of a parapet some edge upstand should be provided to prevent wind blown water spilling over flat roof verges. There is evidence that upstands need to be higher than they often are, **24**. Cases are known where an upstand of 50 mm has been insufficient to prevent soaking of walling below the verge.

Assuming that construction details are adequate to prevent water penetration into a building the consequence of water overspill may be:

1 *Increased risk of deterioration*
  notably to paint finishes;
  decay of non-durable timber fascias or cladding;
  possible trouble from increased risk of frost action on masonry walling.

2 *Disfigurement*
  extra risk of efflorescence on walls;
  permanent streaking, at concentrated run-off positions;
  transient discoloration eg on light-coloured calcium silicate brickwork.

These faults are more likely to be troublesome as a result of frequent relatively small overspills rather than the effect of occasional severe storms. Upstands should therefore be sufficient at least to prevent overspill under general weather conditions. The necessary height of an upstand depends upon site exposure and the shape of the upstand. A vertical or steep angle between upstand and roof is more effective than a low angle form, but, in practice, an angle of about 45° or less is often used in order to avoid sharp changes in direction of roof waterproofing membranes. Upstands at verges also help to prevent loose chippings blowing off the roof.

The above factors make determination of the height of an upstand a matter of judgment but it is suggested that 50 mm should normally be regarded as a minimum requirement when the rise is formed at about 45°, **25**.

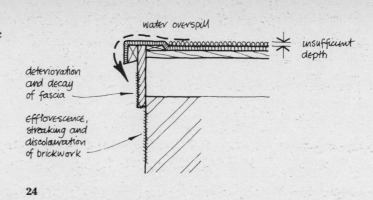

water overspill
insufficient depth
deterioration and decay of fascia
efflorescence, streaking and discolouration of brickwork

24

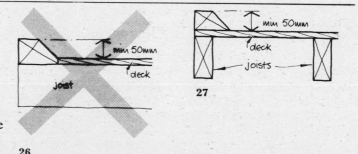

45°
min 50mm upstand
roof finish

25

Upstand details

Support for upstand

If upstands were to occur *only* where joists are at right angles, fixing could be direct to joists with the deck stopping against the upstand, **26**.

An objection to this method is that, unless the deck material is very stiff, deflection occurs; this may cause cracking in the waterproofing along the junction between deck and upstand. The method shown in **27** is therefore preferred even where joists are at right angles.

min 50mm
deck
joist

26

min 50mm
deck
joists

27

With joists parallel the deck is normally carried on the last joist, **27**. Upstand kerbs are then fixed to the deck, or through the deck to the joists.

For simplicity, deck insulation and firring or cross battening are ignored in **26** and **27**.

The effect of roof falls

If it is visually acceptable for upstands to have their top edge sloping to follow roof falls there are few problems. Where, for the sake of appearance, tops of upstands are to be level, fixing problems arise. In the following diagrams it is assumed that a minimum upstand of 50 mm is required and that total roof fall is 100 mm. (For most roof finishes this would mean a roof length not exceeding about 6 m.) It is also assumed that upstands are fixed above any decking and that the top surface of the upstand needs to be 50 mm wide, **28**.

At the low roof position the kerb, as a single softwood member, becomes large and involves wasteful cutting. Significant shrinkage of the kerb member may also occur.

This arrangement, **29**, is more economical than **28**, but the kerb begins to look precarious, liable to warping and difficult to secure against damage, eg from ladders.

The effect of thermal insulation

Where design is of the warm roof type ie with vapour barrier and thermal insulation above the roof deck, the kerb has to be higher. The following examples assume 35 mm for insulation although more might well be used.

The upstand kerb becomes more precarious in **30**, and very liable to twisting on drying out. Note that if decking is kept level, and wedge-shaped insulation is used, the overall size of kerb member would not alter, but the angle fillet would have to be cut to falls and be out of timber 100 mm larger. Where kerbs become as large as this example it may be better to use a framed-up form rather than a solid member.

In the above examples the deck is assumed to be of timber boarding or similar material. If deck and insulation are combined, eg as wood wool or strawboard, and the deck is carried through to the perimeter, secure fixing of the upstand kerb to the joists would be inhibited, **31**.

By stopping the insulating deck against the kerb member, direct kerb to joist fixing is again obtained, but with a further increase in kerb height and the need to provide edge support for the decking, **32**.

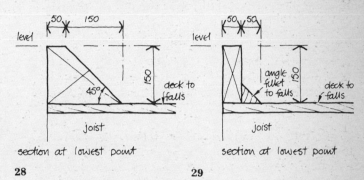

28   **29**

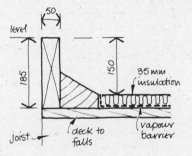

30

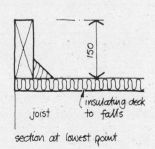

31

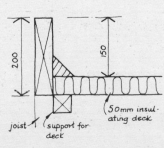

32

The effect of method of obtaining roof falls
Figs **33** to **40** show how conditions for fixing a kerb are
affected by various methods used for obtaining roof falls.
The introduction of firring, and even more of
cross battening, reduces the feasibility of obtaining secure
fixing of the kerb by nailing or screwing.

Conclusions
Although the problem is a very elementary one it has been
examined at some length. The following conclusions may be
drawn:

1 Early design decisions about removal of water and general
joist arrangement and the direction of roof falls may result
in problems in later detailing (see details 18 and 19, pages
80-88).

2 A single 'typical' section will not provide sufficient
safeguard to avoid some nasty site problems which may cause
delay and would probably result in claims for extras. It is
essential to detail all variations of the kerb arrangement and
to cover special aspects, eg a kerb end meeting a cross wall.

3 Secure fixing of kerbs, with adequate upstands and level
tops, presents difficulties. Simple nailing would be adequate
in only a few of the above examples.

Fall and joists parallel to kerb

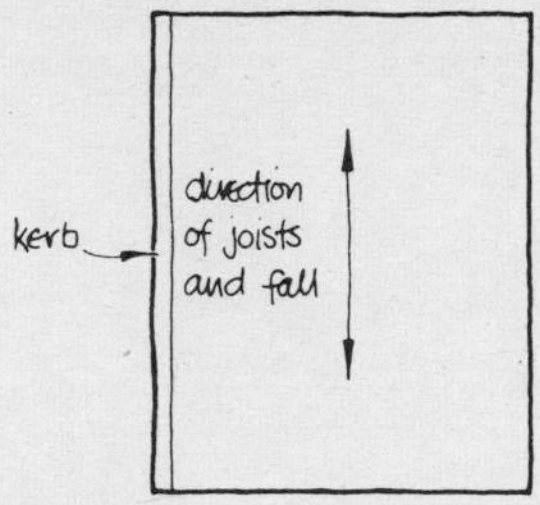

Joists at right angles to kerb ; fall parallel

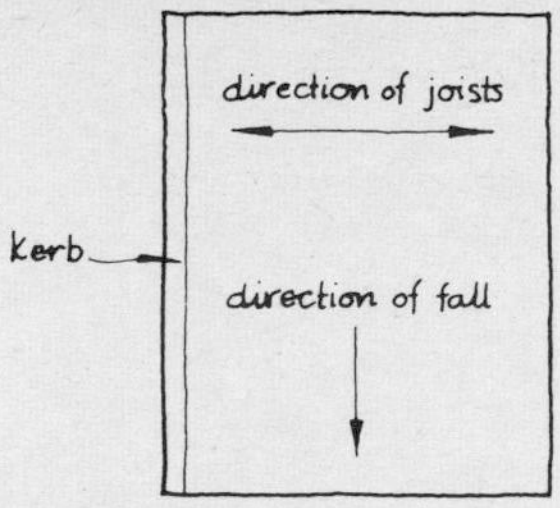

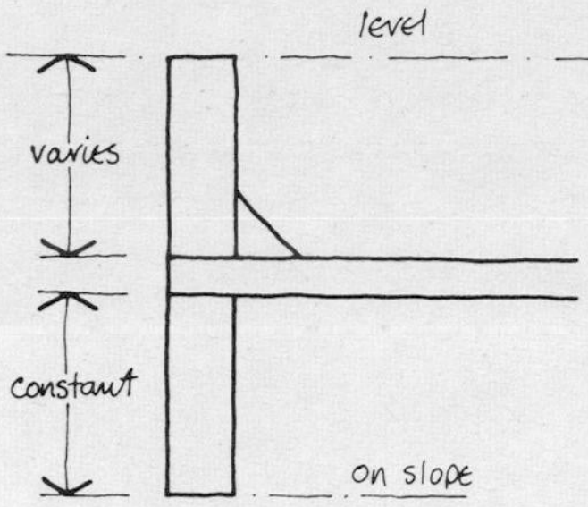

joists laid to falls
33

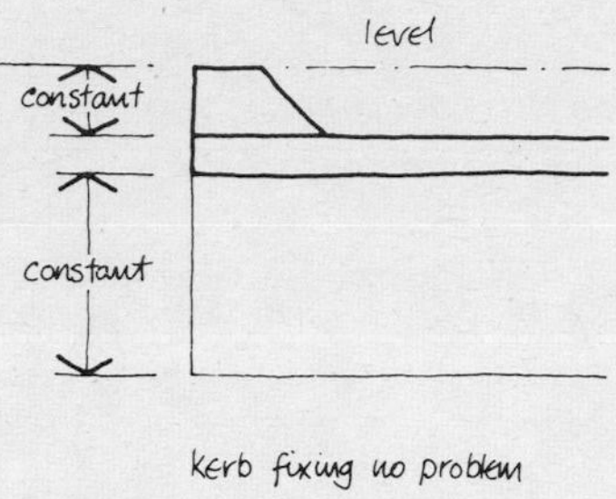

kerb fixing no problem
joists laid to falls
34

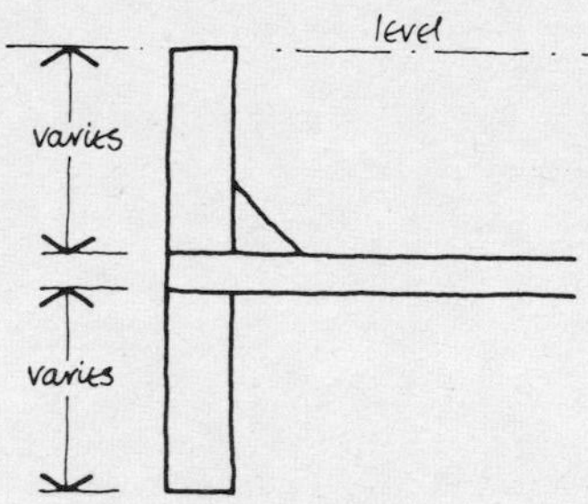

joists cut to falls
35

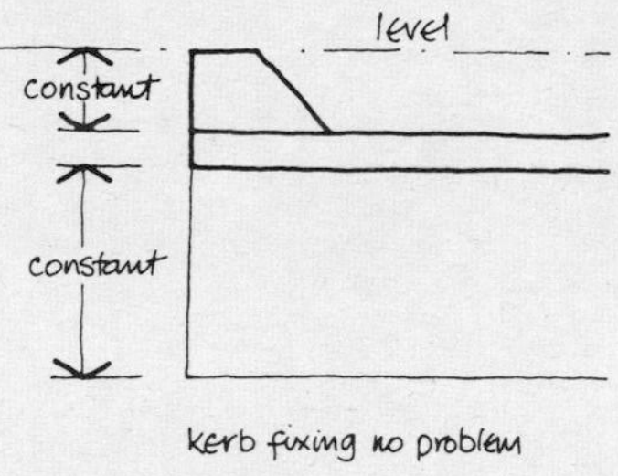

kerb fixing no problem
joists cut to falls
36

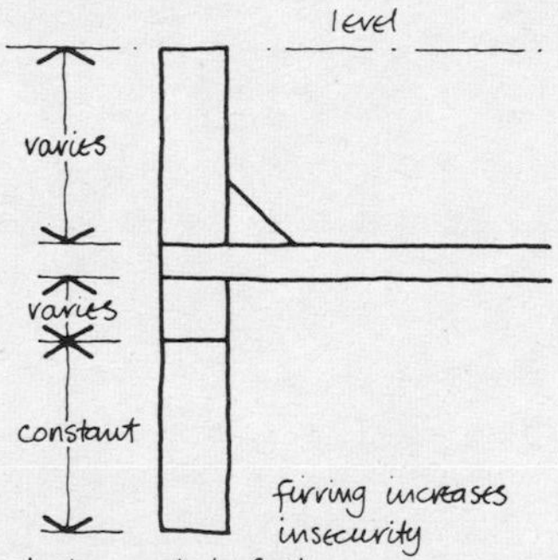

furring increases insecurity
firring cut to falls
37

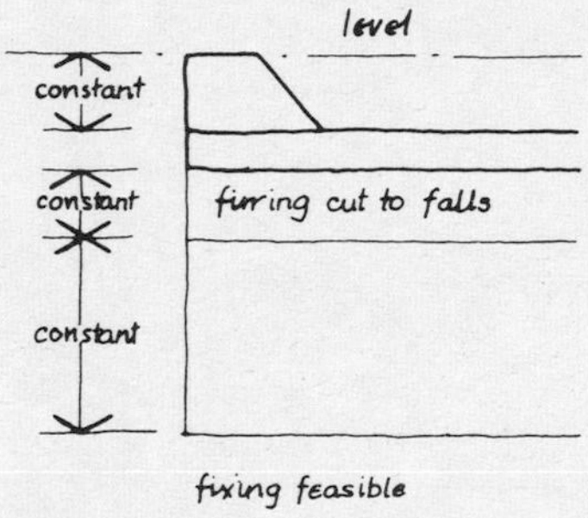

furring cut to falls
fixing feasible
furring cut to falls
38

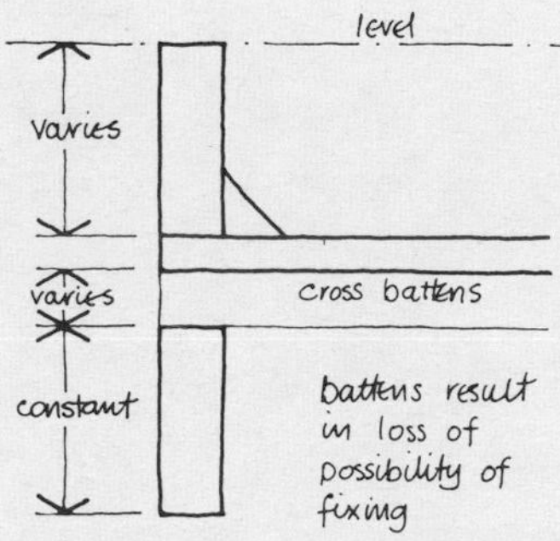

cross battens
battens result in loss of possibility of fixing
falls from cross battens varying in thickness
39

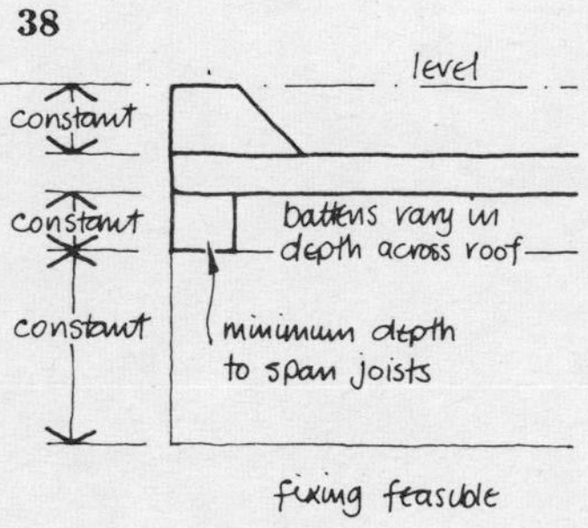

battens vary in depth across roof
minimum depth to span joists
fixing feasible
cross battens cut to falls
40

Fixing recommendations

It is fairly common practice for nail fixings, and sometimes screw fixings, to be left to the contractor with a 'cover' specification such as 'securely fix'. In such cases the site supervisor should have at least some idea of what to regard as acceptable. The following examples are intended to give this sort of guidance.

For kerbs not exceeding 50 mm in thickness, opposed skew nailing, with 100 mm headless nails well pushed down at about 500 mm centres, should be adequate when fixing is to a firm base, **41**.

Pre-drilling and vertical screwing at about 500 mm centres can be used where a screw would ensure a 'bite' of not less than 35 mm into a firm base, and where the whole length of the screw is through firm material, **42**. Fixing centres should depend on the total construction, eg on whether or not extra stability is obtained from a fascia applied to the basic structure. If 150 mm maximum screw length is assumed and the deck is 25 mm, the kerb height would be 135 mm.

Skew-angled nail fixing plus care in providing lateral support from an angle fillet securely fixed to deck and kerb needs very careful workmanship, but is only likely to be effective if any joists parallel to the kerb are increased to 75 mm, **43**. Kerbs might then be up to 150 mm in height.

For kerbs more than 135 mm in height some form of metal support is necessary, **44**. Galvanised iron angle straps of 35 to 40 mm × 3 to 5 mm section should be screw-fixed to kerb and firm decking at about 500 mm centres.

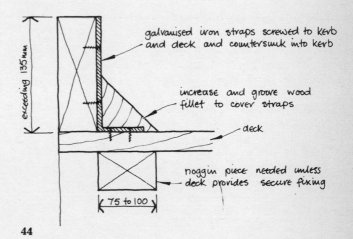

opposed skew nailing

50

wood or other firm deck not less than 25 mm thick

41

counterbored

washer

vertical screw

deck

joist

42

min 50 mm fillet nailed to kerb and deck

deck

joist

43

exceeding 135 mm

galvanised iron straps screwed to kerb and deck and countersunk into kerb

increase and groove wood fillet to cover straps

deck

noggin piece needed unless deck provides secure fixing

75 to 100

44

Verge drip details

With an upstand verge which contains most of the roof water serious wetting of walling will not occur, but detailing of the edge trim still has a disfiguring effect.

Where asphalt or a sheet membrane is carried over a kerb and turned down to form a drip, the drip should be well forward of the fascia, **45, 46**. The bottom of the asphalt or felt drip should be kept as level as possible to avoid concentrated drip-off points.

There may be objections to details **45** and **46** on grounds of appearance. It is also questionable whether or not, even when reinforced as shown, an asphalt finish over the top of three pieces of timber would remain undamaged. A detail such as **47** would be better.

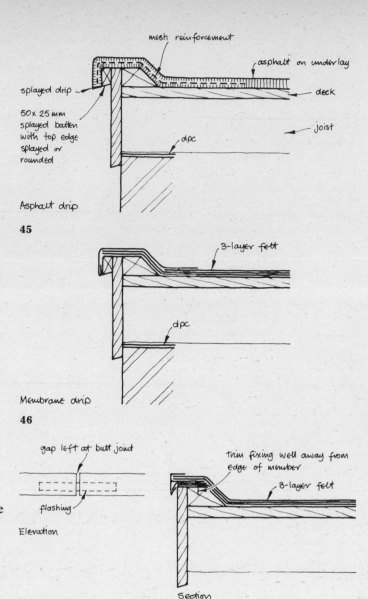

Asphalt drip

45

Membrane drip

46

When the appearance of the roof finish exposed as a vertical drip is unacceptable a thin metal flashing could be inserted as an alternative, but it is now more usual to finish with a proprietary edge trim of aluminium or plastic. Care should be taken to check that the kerb dimensions provide for correct fixing, ie that holes through the trim will not be too near the edge of the kerb member. To avoid distortion of the trim by thermal expansion fixing should be through slotted holes.

Adjacent lengths of trim are butt jointed in order to keep alignment. These joints should not be tight butted. Manufacturers should advise on what joint gap is appropriate for their material. A simple butt joint allows water through and is in the position most likely to cause concentrated run off with consequential streaking on the fascia or wall. While it is difficult to eliminate this completely, the risk of disfigurement is reduced if a flashing strip is inserted at joints. Some manufacturers provide these as part of the trim 'kit'.

With a multiple layer membrane roof the bottom layer is sometimes detailed to project and turn down into the metal trim, **48**. If achieved as drawn this takes care of the butt joint problem but it is doubtful whether in practice the membrane would be finished accurately enough to be effective.

A detail like that shown in **49** is sometimes used where the roof membrane is covered by a metal capping. But note that:

1 the kerb must *everywhere* be at least 150 mm high (therefore higher in parts because of falls) to prevent snow entry;

2 wind could blow water up under the capping and might get through into the construction unless workmanship is exceptionally good.

gap left at butt joint

flashing

Elevation

trim fixing well away from edge of member

3-layer felt

Section

47

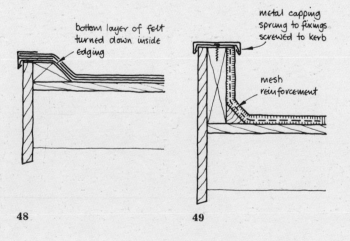

bottom layer of felt turned down inside edging

metal capping sprung to fixings screwed to kerb

mesh reinforcement

48

49

21

Parapets in masonry construction

Criteria

Parapets should be designed for:
Safety: height and structural stability.
Durability: choice and usage of materials. Appropriate construction, eg movement joints.
Appearance including prevention of disfigurement, which may occur without causing serious deterioration.
Avoidance of damp penetration to other parts of a structure.

This detail is concerned primarily with methods of preventing undue wetting of parapets, and with the prevention of water penetration from parapets to walls beneath or into adjacent roofing.

Copings

Coping material

Copings are exposed to extremes of temperature and a frequent cycle of wetting and drying. They need to have a greater resistance to frost than is necessary for ordinary walling and they should be resistant to sulphate action.

Water entry through copings

Water may enter through the coping material or through joints. Thermal movement especially is likely to be considerable and will almost inevitably result in water penetration through jointing of bricks, stones or precast concrete units.

As a precaution against damage to coping units and joints the top should slope to assist water run-off, **1**.

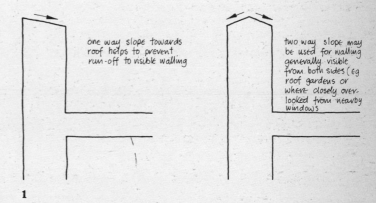

one way slope towards roof helps to prevent run-off to visible walling

two way slope may be used for walling generally visible from both sides (eg roof gardens or where closely overlooked from nearby windows)

1

Water run-off from coping may add to the risk of damage and often causes disfigurement to walling below the coping, especially if the coping material is slightly soluble, **2**. White staining from limestone and from some precast concrete frequently occurs.

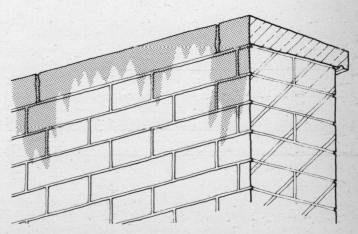

2

Protection against run-off should include a projection and drip at least on the discharge edge, **3**.

Where the coping material is liable to stain walling beneath, projecting drips should be on both sides, even if the coping slopes one way only, **4**.
For masonry type copings a projection of not less than 40 mm is necessary.

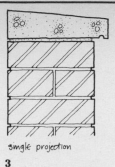

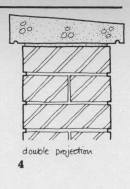

single projection

3

double projection

4

Dpc beneath copings

Unless the coping material *and its joints* are completely impervious a dpc beneath the coping is essential, **5**.
The dpc should extend *at least* to full width of the wall. Because any material above a dpc will become wet, it is desirable to locate the dpc immediately beneath the coping, although a disadvantage is that movement in the coping may loosen individual units. It is probably for this reason that, where copings are of small units such as bricks, the dpc is sometimes placed one or two courses down. Where this is done the materials above dpc should all be resistant to the sulphate action and frost damage liable to occur in situations of severe exposure; clay bricks, for example, should be to BS 3921 'special' quality. If a sheet material dpc is used it should be fully bedded, with mortar above and below, and preferably should be of a type with a rough or granular surface which helps to ensure good bonding.

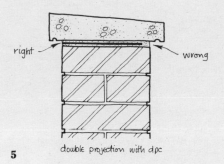

right — wrong

double projection with dpc

5

Because mortar jointing in the projecting part of copings is very liable to fail, through coping movement, dribble marks are especially likely to occur on walling beneath joints, **6**.

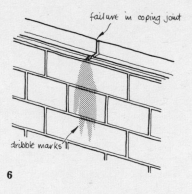

failure in coping joint

dribble marks

6

Projecting the under-coping dpc helps to prevent this but with flexible sheet material it is difficult to ensure either a turn-down or a neat appearance, especially at the necessary lapped joints, **7**.

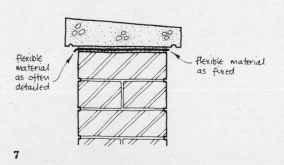

flexible material as often detailed — flexible material as fixed

7

In several European countries normal practice is to use a stiff zinc dpc with pre-formed drips. With this method it is unnecessary for the coping itself to exceed the wall width, **8**. Joints in the metal dpc should be designed to allow some movement and still remain waterproof, either by forming a welted joint or by using an under flashing.

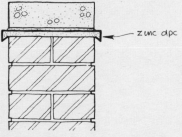

— zinc dpc

8

In cavity walls flexible dpcs will deflect over the cavity. Water will then run along the 'gutter' and may discharge at joints, **9**.

The cavity should be sealed with a sheet of thin rigid material before the dpc is fixed, **10**.

Completely impervious coping materials, such as metals or plastics, are normally in fairly long sections and have high thermal movement which must be allowed for. Unless this movement is accommodated by a welted joint, care should be taken to design a joint detail which is both waterproof and which prevents expansion from buckling the coping. Close butt joints of long sheets should be avoided.

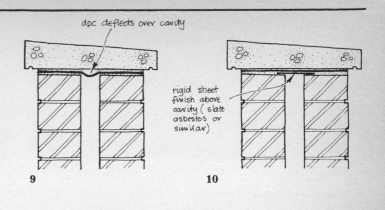

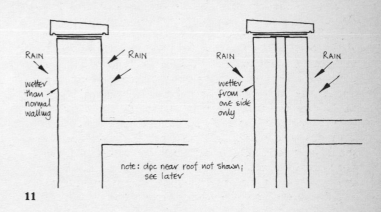

9   **10**

Damp in parapet masonry

Even if rain penetration through the coping can be prevented, parapet walls are usually more exposed to wetting than normal external walling because there is exposure on both sides and, in the case of roof parapets, because they are likely to be exposed to severe wind driven rain, **11**.

Even if walling materials, including mortar, are adequate for frost resistance and freedom from sulphate action or efflorescence, difference in appearance between parapet and wall below may occur. The chance of such disfigurement is appreciably reduced if cavity rather than solid walling is used.

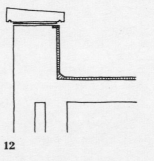

11

A possible alternative to cavity construction is to prevent rain access from the roof side, **12**. With a low parapet it may be feasible to carry the roofing membrane up to the coping dpc. Good adhesion of membrane to wall is essential and a fully secured turn-in beneath the dpc is necessary. Vertical waterproofing cannot easily be protected from effects of the sun. Thermal or other movement in the walling may affect the membrane. This method is *not* recommended for parapets exceeding about 350 mm height to underside of coping, and is considered less satisfactory than a cavity for any situation.

12

The use of cement type rendering as a waterproofing method for this position is *not* recommended, **13**. Parapet movement is likely to cause cracking. Rain access from the front increases risk of frost damage and of sulphate action. Damage to rendering is liable to be unnoticed until it has become very bad.

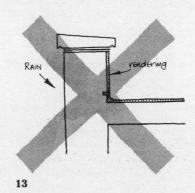

13

Water entry to roof structure or rooms below

With a low parapet, in cavity construction, with a fully effective dpc beneath the coping and with the roof side of the parapet fully waterproofed, the roof structure and rooms below are fully protected, **14**.

In all cases where the roof side of the parapet wall is exposed to rain penetration a dpc must be provided immediately above the roof membrane top-of-skirting level. Either the dpc or a separate flashing must cover the skirting.

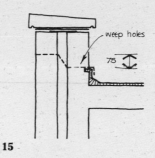

14

With cavity walling, water penetrating the roof side must be prevented from running down the cavity face of the inner leaf by continuing the dpc, stepped up, across the cavity, **15**. Because there is only a small height of wall above the dpc and clearing of mortar droppings is easy, the step up need not exceed 75 mm.

Detail **15** shows the lower dpc stepped down towards the roof. This appears to be the most frequently recommended arrangement and is adopted because any water from the cavity is directed onto the roof rather than onto the face of the wall. Some experienced building supervisors say that, on exposed sites, face water enters the external skin immediately *below* the dpc and is then conveyed down the underside of the dpc to the interior wall. They therefore prefer the dpc to be laid in the reverse direction, **16**. This is a point that should certainly be considered where cavity fill insulation is used.

15

16

If solid parapets are used there is a risk of water penetration to roof structure or rooms from the front. This risk is increased if the wall thickness is reduced above roof bearing level, **17**.

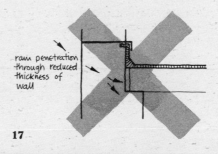

17

Waterproofing of roof to wall junction

In the examples above the arrangement of dpc/roof skirting/roof membrane is shown only in diagrammatic form. A very high proportion of roof leaks occur because of poor workmanship of the wall-to-roof waterproofing. This section deals with roof finishes of mastic asphalt or flexible sheet membranes of either single or multiple layer type, but for simplicity the membranes are in all cases drawn as a single thick line.

The main roof area should be designed to prevent unacceptable stress in the membrane being transferred from roof structure movement. Even with that precaution the turn-up position from roof to skirting needs to be strong. A splayed corner is usually formed. Solid asphalt has a splayed fillet (or core), **18**.

Flexible membranes use a timber or cement mortar splay, dependent upon roof construction, **19**.

A flexible angle underlay is a possible alternative to an angle fillet for flexible membrane finishes, **20**. It should be used only if the roofing specialist contractor prefers to do it this way.

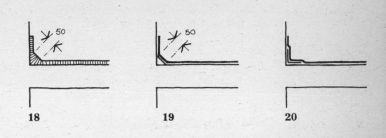

18   **19**   **20**

A very large number of flat roof leaks occur because of poor design or poor workmanship at skirtings. There are three basic methods:

1 Continuous membrane for roof, skirting and wall dpc, **21**. This is only possible if done before upper part of wall is built (which may be inconvenient). Sometimes recommended with asphalt but not recommended for flexible sheet membranes. With asphalt it is most appropriate for solid wall parapets. Cavity walls would need a further material across the cavity.

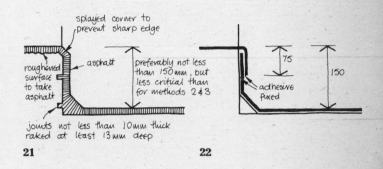

21   **22**

2 Separate wall dpc of flexible membrane turned down and adhesive fixed to skirting, **22**.
This is only feasible if done before the upper part of the wall is built; a wall dpc left projecting for later adhesion to skirting is too likely to be damaged.

It is cheaper than method 3 below, and avoids risk of separate cover flashing being insecurely fixed. But there is more risk of damage from roof/wall movement. Skirting should be at least 150 mm high and dpc flashing seal should be at least 75 mm.

This method is not advised as the dpc material may not be suited to exposure or may be difficult to shape without damage, and the adhesive fixing may not prove permanent.

Codes of practice and other recommendations do not call for a splay joint to ease the bend into the wall, but for some materials this might help to reduce risk of cracking.

Note that for method 1 the whole system may be completed at one time and therefore by a single contractor. If the waterproofing is delayed the incomplete wall is very open to damage by water entry. A fully effective temporary protection should be specified and its provision ensured by site inspection.

3 A separate flashing unit inserted beneath the wall
flashing and lapping the skirting, **23**.
If in metal the flashing is unbonded to skirting, and
roof/wall movement is less critical. It is more expensive
than methods 1 and 2. Height to flashing should be at least
75 mm. (Watch for reduction due to roof slopes.) Suitable
for asphalt or sheet membrane roofing. Flashing frequently
becomes displaced because of bad fixing. In theory the
parapet wall with dpc may be completed prior to roof
membrane and skirting but 1, it is difficult to ensure good
fixing of the flashing if delayed until roofing is completed,
and the wall dpc is likely to be damaged, and 2, if fixed
prior to roof membrane a *stiff* metal flashing will be
inconvenient to the roofer, and may be loosened during the
manipulation necessary to allow skirting to be applied.

If flashing is done by general contractor the work should
follow immediately after roofing unless the flashing has
been fixed at the same time as the wall dpc. In the latter
case the general contractor should immediately follow the
roofer to dress the flashing to position and check against
damage.

If method 3 is used in conjunction with asphalt the asphalt
should be turned into a wall chase, **24**. A chase of at least
25 mm × 25 mm is needed. Raking of a normal wall joint
is *not* sufficient. The metal flashing is wedged under a dpc
at higher level.

Very similar conditions apply at the junction of flat roofs
with a higher building, but usually without the option of
carrying out all the waterproofing while the wall is at dpc
level (see detail 16, page 72).

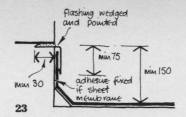

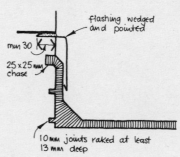

22

Pitched roofs: eaves

Keeping out the rain

Faults

With pitched roofs, trouble from water in the wrong place
is most likely to occur at the eaves, **1**. Faults include:
1 Failure to discharge main run-off water correctly into
gutters.
2 Failure to ensure that water reaching the top surface of
sarking is carried clear of roof or wall structure.
3 Dampness caused by condensation. Condensation within
pitched roof spaces is likely to be worst near the eaves.

It is worth noting that faults of types 1 and 2 have
probably increased in frequency following the trend
towards low pitched roofs. One of the factors influencing
condensation is roof space ventilation.

This detail covers faults 1 and 2. The effect of eaves
detailing upon condensation will be covered on page 107.

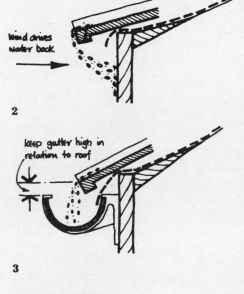

1

Main water run-off

Water dripping from the roof edge tends to be blown back,
towards the fascia, **2**. This is especially so with thick edged
tiles.

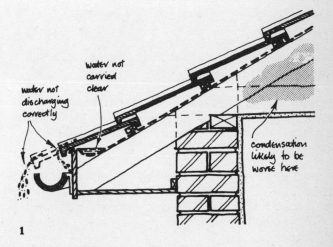

2

Gutters should be fixed as high as possible in relation to
edge of roof, **3**. Gutter falls increase gutter capacity, but
excessive falls in long gutters result in the low end being
too far below roof edge. Falls should be 10 mm for 5 m
to 6 m length.

3

The edge of the roof covering should project well across the
gutter, **4**. With very small gutters there must inevitably
be some compromise between projecting the roof too little,
and as a result having water blown back over the back of
the gutter, and projecting too much, with resultant
overshoot of water during heavy rain. A look at a range of
illustrations in text books and brochures discloses
remarkable differences.

Normally tiles or slates should overhang the gutter by
40 mm. With very small gutters this might perhaps be cut
to 35 mm. It is better to risk occasional overspill at the
front than frequent blow-back onto the fascia.

Even with better detailing, fascias are liable to be wetter than
most exposed vertical surfaces. Timber fascias should
always be treated with preservative. Painted fascias should
receive full painting *before* gutters are fixed. They will
seldom, if ever, be properly painted subsequently.

4

The bottom edge of timber fascias is especially vulnerable
to rot. A splayed bottom edge helps in reducing the risk by
encouraging water to drip off the bottom outer edge, **5**.
The outer edge should be softened to prevent paint film
cracking and flaking.

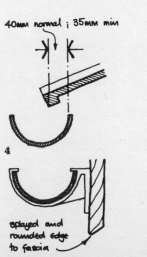

5

Water from top of sarking

It should be accepted that some penetration of driving rain or snow through tiled roofs will occur at times. If correctly laid, sarking is an effective second line of defence. It is essential that water running down the top surface of the sarking should have an easy outlet at the eaves. This does not always occur.

Sheer carelessness in workmanship and supervision sometimes results in sarking stopping short of the fascia, **6**, or short of the gutter beyond.

Ideally the sarking should project and turn down into the gutter, **7**. At least the material should come over and beyond the front edge of the fascia.

A less obvious trouble occurs where low pitched roofs result in the sarking becoming horizontal, or even sagging below the top edge of the fascia. Illustration **8** appeared not long ago in a series of details from a very reputable source. The sarking is drawn almost horizontal and may well sag between supports. When roof pitch makes a nearly flat finish inevitable, the sarking should be fully supported over that area by boarding rather than by fillets only at joist positions.

Any joint, or accidental damage on the almost horizontal sarking, would lead to trouble. There is the added risk that some rain or snow may be blown up under the roof to this area. Cases are known where, in cold weather, accumulated water on flat sarking has frozen and caused a blockage, thus trapping water from higher up with resultant leaking. With very low pitched roofs it is difficult to avoid almost horizontal sarking immediately behind the fascia. This makes careful supervision very important *immediately* before tiling starts.

Detail drawings, and the work executed before battens are covered, should be checked to ensure that at no point is there any possibility of water accumulating along the length of battens, as this will lead to subsequent rotting of the batten and/or water penetration in the roof, **9**.

Sarking should sag slightly between rafters, and in cases where continuous members are at right angles to rafters (eg roof boarding) counter battens should be used.

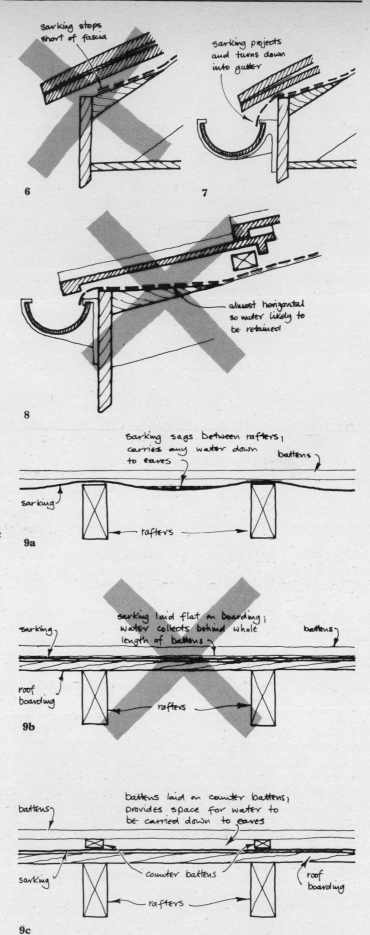

sarking stops short of fascia

6

sarking projects and turns down into gutter

7

almost horizontal so water likely to be retained

8

sarking sags between rafters, carries any water down to eaves
battens
sarking
rafters

9a

sarking laid flat on boarding; water collects behind whole length of battens
sarking
battens
roof boarding
rafters

9b

battens laid on counter battens; provides space for water to be carried down to eaves
battens
sarking
counter battens
rafters
roof boarding

9c

Effect on condensation
The problem

Ventilation is only one of a number of factors that affect the incidence of condensation in roof spaces, but since the difference in conditions which cause serious trouble and those which are satisfactory can be quite small, the degree of ventilation may be a decisive factor. General points to note are shown in **10** and include:

1 Tiled or slated roofs are now almost always relatively well sealed by sarking, so the general roof space gets much less fortuitous ventilation than do many old roofs.

2 The volume of roof space is reduced where the roof has a low pitch. Water vapour reaching the roof space therefore has a greater immediate effect upon roof space air moisture content.

3 With low pitched roofs the space near the eaves is particularly restricted and, in the absence of eaves ventilation, may become stagnant and therefore conducive to timber rot.

In recent years it has become commonplace for technical information publications to include recommendations for deliberate ventilation at the eaves. A look through information from a number of reputable sources suggests that there is no general agreement on exactly what should be done. The following illustrations show some of the rather confusing variations that have appeared. The illustrations and their descriptions are reproduced in their original form. The comments have been added to draw attention to important points.

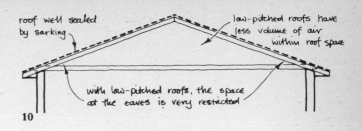

roof well sealed by sarking

low-pitched roofs have less volume of air within roof space

with low-pitched roofs, the space at the eaves is very restricted

10

Examples of published information
Tiled or slated roof over 20° pitch
Explanation of original drawing

In the circumstances shown in **11** there is no need for a vapour barrier at ceiling level as the ventilation of the roof space is sufficient to maintain moisture below saturation level.

In exposed areas care should be taken in laying of roofing felt in order to prevent rain or snow driving into the roof space.

Comments
 ● Area of ventilation is equivalent to a continuous gap 1 mm wide. Could the soffit be fixed without providing at least this?
 ● Top of wall cavity is sealed. Possibly done for purpose of spreading the roof load but has the effect of preventing cavity moist air rising directly to the eaves timber.
 ● Ceiling insulation stops at inner wall face and therefore does not impede eaves ventilation reaching main roof space.
 ● No special vapour check at ceiling is indicated.

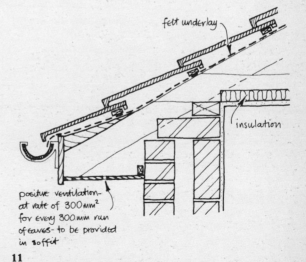

felt underlay

insulation

positive ventilation at rate of 300mm² for every 300mm run of eaves- to be provided in soffit

11

Tiled or slated roof over 20° pitch: recommendations for Scotland
Explanation of original drawing
In the circumstances shown in **12** there is no need for a vapour barrier as the natural ventilation of the roof space is sufficient to maintain moisture vapour below saturation level.

Comments
- No positive eaves ventilation shown but ventilation assumed to occur (compare **11**).
- No ceiling vapour check 'because natural ventilation of roof space is sufficient'.
- Ceiling insulation carried part way across wall but still does not prevent eaves ventilation reaching main roof space.
- Top of cavity wall not sealed. Probably the external rendering will reduce rain penetration through the outer wall but, as cavity air is still likely to have high moisture content at times, it seems curious that the cavity is not sealed.

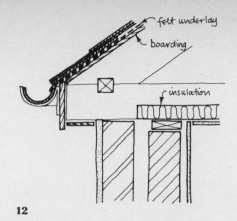

12

Tiled or slated roof below 20° pitch
Explanation of original drawing
Low pitched roofs do not provide sufficient volume of air to disperse vapour penetrating from the rooms below. A vapour check is therefore required at ceiling level, **13**. In Scotland and other areas of high relative humidity it is not desirable to ventilate the roof space.

Comments
- Except for the addition of the ceiling vapour check, this is similar to **11**.
- The reference to areas of high humidity is not explicit. In most areas, including the South, winter air is at high relative humidity for much of the time. This type of weather may persist for longer in Scotland and some other regions.
- Not everyone would agree with the recommendation to omit ventilation. In fact some fortuitous ventilation probably occurs anyway, and it may be that this proves adequate (see the comment to illustration **11**).

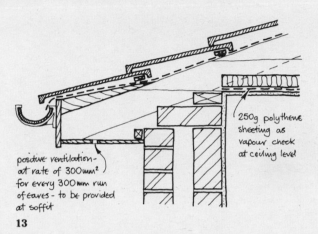

13

Low pitched tile roof
Explanation of original drawing
In this example, **14**, the cavity is open to the roof space.

Comments
- No specific reference to eaves ventilation.
- Top of cavity not sealed.
- Ceiling is foil-backed plasterboard. With other insulation materials in contact, the reflective thermal insulation value of the foil is lost. Presumably therefore the foil is intended to form a vapour check. If this is so it seems odd to allow moist air from the wall cavity to rise unimpeded to the roof space.

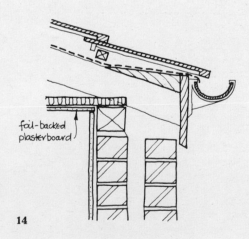

14

Steep pitch tile roof
Explanation of original drawing
Example **15** has a sealed cavity but with eaves ventilation.

Comments
- Ventilation holes specified by size but no information on how many.
- If positive ventilation is desired why spend money on tongued and grooved joint at soffit/fascia, when a gap between a plain edged soffit and fascia will provide ventilation?
- Note that no ceiling or other thermal insulation is shown.

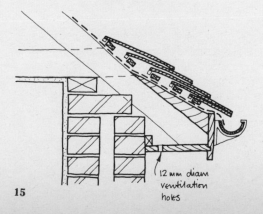

15

Open and closed cavities
Explanation of original drawing
The building constructed as shown in **16a** had decaying eaves timbers within four years. Rooms showed some signs of condensation. The defect was attributed to moist air rising from open wall cavity plus some water vapour passing through ceiling, all resulting in build-up of damp condition in airtight eaves.

Construction as in **16b** was suggested as a suitable alternative, with eaves soffit ventilation of 1000 mm² per metre run, and a closed top to the wall cavity. Also moisture penetration through the ceiling to be prevented.

Comments
● Having ventilated the eaves and sealed the wall cavity, it seems odd to have carried brickwork up as beam filling. This would, if solidly carried out, prevent the eaves ventilation reaching the main roof space.
● There is no specific advice on how to prevent water vapour from rooms penetrating the ceiling. A vapour check at ceiling level is presumably intended. Ceiling vapour checks are not completely effective barriers, and for this reason the main roof space would have been better if open to benefit from the eaves ventilation.

Roof ventilation
Explanation of original drawing
If roof space is ventilated, insulation should be at ceiling level, **8**. For good ventilation allow 2000 mm² of opening per metre run of eaves. The ceiling should be free from gaps or holes.

Comments
● Ventilation recommendation is for twice the quantity suggested by other examples (**11, 13, 15**).
● No proviso about not ventilating in Scotland or similar weather regions.
● Reference to the ceiling being free from gaps or holes presumably does not imply the higher requirement of including a positive vapour check at ceiling level.

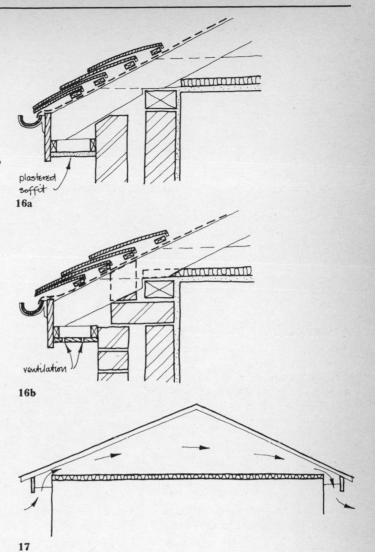

plastered soffit

16a

ventilation

16b

17

Summary

It seems that there is a need for more reliable information based on feedback information. Pending this (and as summarised in **18**) it is suggested that:

1 Tops of wall cavities should be sealed.

2 With low pitched roofs ceilings should provide a reasonably good vapour check. This might be in the form of a layer of impervious material above the ceiling or, where ceiling is free from joints, might be obtained by surface finish of a gloss oil paint or similar.

3 If all roof timbers are not treated with preservative at least those at the eaves should have some protection.

4 Eaves design should not deliberately prevent eaves ventilation, eg the rendered soffit of drawing **16a**. In most forms of construction fortuitous ventilation at the eaves seems likely to provide the amount of inlet area of the various recommendations (1 to 2 mm² per mm run of eaves).

5 Where a roof has gable ends these are sometimes accepted as the positions in which to locate ventilation openings. This may usually be quite effective but for low pitched roofs where stagnant air near the eaves is a particular risk, some eaves ventilation is probably worth having.

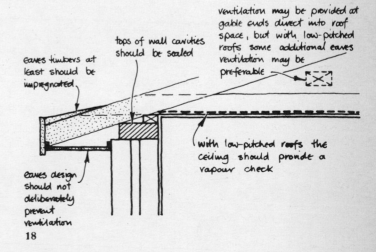

Eaves timbers at least should be impregnated

tops of wall cavities should be sealed

ventilation may be provided at gable ends direct into roof space, but with low-pitched roofs some additional eaves ventilation may be preferable

with low-pitched roofs the ceiling should provide a vapour check

eaves design should not deliberately prevent ventilation

18

Coventry University Library